AMAZON RETURN PALLETS

TURNING RETURNS INTO CASH

TYLER MORGAN

© . All rights reserved.

No part of this book may be reproduced or utilized in any form or by any means, electronic or mechanical, including photocopying, recording, or by any information storage and retrieval system, without permission in writing from the publisher.

Published by Tyler Morgan

Disclaimer: *"This book is not endorsed by, affiliated with, or sponsored by Amazon.com, Inc. or any of its subsidiaries."*

CONTENTS

INTRODUCTION 4

CHAPTER 1: INTRODUCTION TO AMAZON RETURN PALLETS 6

CHAPTER 2: SOURCING RETURN PALLETS 19

CHAPTER 3: ASSESSING RETURN PALLET VALUE 31

CHAPTER 4: NEGOTIATING DEALS 43

CHAPTER 5: LOGISTICS AND STORAGE 55

CHAPTER 6: PREPARING ITEMS FOR RESALE 67

CHAPTER 7: SELLING PLATFORMS 79

CHAPTER 8: MARKETING STRATEGIES 92

CHAPTER 9: CUSTOMER SERVICE EXCELLENCE 105

CHAPTER 10: LEGAL AND ETHICAL CONSIDERATIONS 118

CHAPTER 11: SCALING YOUR BUSINESS 130

CHAPTER 12: REAL-LIFE SUCCESS STORIES 143

CHAPTER 13: FUTURE TRENDS IN RETURN PALLETS 155

INTRODUCTION

In the fast-paced world of e-commerce, returns are an inevitable part of doing business. For many, these returns represent a logistical headache and a loss of revenue. However, for the savvy entrepreneur, they present a golden opportunity. Welcome to the intriguing world of Amazon return pallets—a domain where returned items are not just discarded or overlooked but are instead transformed into profitable ventures.

This book aims to demystify the often misunderstood and underutilized market of Amazon return pallets. Whether you're a seasoned reseller or a curious newcomer, this comprehensive guide will provide you with the knowledge and tools needed to turn these returns into cash. We will explore the ins and outs of acquiring return pallets, evaluating their contents, and reselling them for profit. The focus will be on practical strategies that you can implement immediately, regardless of your level of experience.

One of the key features of this book is its geographic specificity. While the market for return pallets is global, the opportunities and challenges can vary significantly depending on your location.

You'll discover how to identify reputable suppliers, navigate the purchasing process, and assess the potential profitability of different types of pallets. We will also delve into the legal and logistical considerations you need to be aware of, ensuring that your venture is not only profitable but also compliant with local regulations.

In addition to the practical advice, this book is filled with real-life case studies and success stories from entrepreneurs who have turned Amazon return pallets into thriving businesses. These stories serve as both inspiration and proof that with the right approach, anyone can succeed in this lucrative market.

Prepare to delve into a world where returned items are not just remnants of failed transactions but are instead the building blocks of a profitable enterprise. This book will equip you with everything you need to know to start turning Amazon returns into cash, no matter where you are located.

Chapter 1: Introduction to Amazon Return Pallets

UNDERSTANDING RETURN PALLETS

Return pallets are a fascinating and integral part of the modern e-commerce ecosystem, particularly within the expansive domain of Amazon. At their core, these pallets are essentially collections of returned items that have been consolidated for resale. They serve as a critical solution for managing the vast number of returns that occur in the online retail world. Understanding the nuances of return pallets can offer significant insights into both the logistical challenges and the potential opportunities they present.

Amazon, one of the largest online marketplaces, handles an immense volume of transactions daily. With such high activity, it is inevitable that a substantial number of products are returned. These returns can occur for a myriad of reasons, ranging from buyer's remorse and incorrect sizing to damaged goods or simply a change of mind. When items are sent back, Amazon categorizes and processes them, often resulting in the creation of return pallets.

One of the primary aspects to grasp about return pallets is the diversity of their contents. They can include anything from electronics and clothing to home goods and toys. This assortment makes them particularly appealing to resellers who are willing to take a chance on the mixed nature of the items. However, this diversity also means that the condition of the products can vary widely. Some items may be in pristine, unopened condition, while others might be slightly used or even damaged. The unpredictability is part of what makes return pallets both a risk and a potential reward.

Another critical element to consider is the categorization and grading process. Amazon, along with other third-party liquidation companies, often sorts and grades the returned items based on their condition. Categories might include "like new," "open box," "used," and "for parts or not working." This grading system helps potential buyers assess the risk involved in purchasing a particular pallet. For instance, a pallet labeled as "like new" is likely to contain items that have minimal wear and are closer to their original condition, whereas a "for parts or not working" pallet might be more suited for those who are skilled in repairs and refurbishments.

The economic implications of return pallets are also noteworthy. For Amazon, these pallets provide a way to recoup some of the losses associated with returns. Instead of storing or disposing of returned items, which can be costly, selling them in bulk allows for a quicker turnover and recapture of some value. For resellers and small business owners, purchasing return pallets can be a cost-effective method to acquire inventory. The lower price point of these pallets, compared to buying new merchandise, can significantly improve profit margins if the items are resold successfully.

Additionally, the rise of return pallets has given birth to a niche market and community. Online forums, social media groups, and dedicated websites have emerged, where individuals share their experiences, tips, and strategies for dealing with return pallets. This community aspect not only provides support but also fosters a sense of camaraderie among those navigating the challenges and rewards of this unique aspect of retail.

Understanding return pallets involves recognizing the intricate balance between risk and opportunity. The variability in the condition and type of items, the grading system, and the economic benefits all play crucial roles in shaping the landscape of this fascinating market. For those willing to delve into the world of return pallets, the potential for discovery and profit is substantial, albeit accompanied by a degree of uncertainty.

WHY AMAZON?

Amidst the sprawling landscape of e-commerce, Amazon stands as a towering behemoth, a titan that has redefined the way the world shops. The allure of Amazon is multifaceted, drawing in sellers and buyers alike with its promise of unparalleled reach, efficiency, and innovation. For those venturing into the realm of return pallets, understanding why Amazon is the preferred marketplace is crucial.

Amazon's vast network is one of its most compelling attributes. With millions of active users spanning the globe, it offers a platform where goods can be moved quickly and efficiently. This extensive customer base ensures that products, even those from return pallets, have a high likelihood of finding a new home. The sheer volume of transactions on Amazon means that there is always a demand for a wide variety of items, from electronics to clothing, making it an ideal marketplace for reselling returned goods.

The technological prowess of Amazon cannot be overlooked. Its sophisticated algorithms and data analytics provide sellers with insights that were once unimaginable. These tools allow sellers to optimize their listings, set competitive prices, and target the right audience. For those dealing in return pallets, this means maximizing the value of each item and ensuring that nothing goes to waste. Amazon's commitment to technological innovation ensures that sellers are always equipped with the latest tools to stay ahead in a competitive market.

Amazon's reputation for customer service is another significant factor. Buyers trust Amazon, knowing that their purchases are protected and that any issues will be resolved promptly. This trust extends to the secondary market of return pallets. Buyers are more willing to purchase items, even those that are refurbished or returned, when they know that Amazon's robust customer service policies back their transactions. This trust translates into higher sales and fewer returns, benefiting sellers immensely.

The logistical capabilities of Amazon are unparalleled. Its state-of-the-art fulfillment centers, combined with an efficient distribution network, ensure that products are delivered swiftly and reliably. For sellers of return pallets, this means that once an item is sold, it can be shipped out with minimal delay, enhancing customer satisfaction and fostering repeat business. The option to use

Amazon's Fulfillment by Amazon (FBA) service further simplifies the process, allowing sellers to focus on sourcing and listing products rather than worrying about storage and shipping logistics.

Another critical aspect is the diversity of Amazon's marketplace. It caters to a vast array of niches and product categories, allowing sellers to find their unique space. Whether dealing in high-end electronics or everyday household items, there is a place for every product on Amazon. This diversity ensures that sellers of return pallets can experiment with different types of goods, finding what works best for them and adapting their strategies accordingly.

Amazon's commitment to sustainability also plays a role. By providing a platform for the resale of returned goods, Amazon promotes a circular economy, reducing waste and encouraging the reuse of products. This aligns with the growing consumer preference for sustainable shopping options, making it easier for sellers to market their return pallet items as eco-friendly choices.

In essence, the magnetism of Amazon lies in its ability to provide a comprehensive, efficient, and trustworthy platform for sellers. Its vast reach, technological edge, logistical expertise, and commitment to customer satisfaction make it the ideal marketplace for those looking to capitalize on the potential of return pallets.

TYPES OF RETURN PALLETS

Return pallets from Amazon are a fascinating and often undervalued aspect of the retail giant's ecosystem. They come in various types, each offering a unique blend of products and opportunities for those who venture into purchasing them. Understanding these types is crucial for maximizing the value and utility derived from these pallets.

General Merchandise pallets are among the most common types of return pallets available. These pallets encompass a broad range of products, from electronics and small appliances to home goods and toys. The diversity in these pallets means there is a little bit of everything, making them ideal for sellers who prefer variety. The condition of items in general merchandise pallets can vary widely, from brand-new items still in their original packaging to slightly used or refurbished products. This variability can be both a challenge and an opportunity, as it requires meticulous sorting but also offers the chance to find high-value items at a fraction of their retail price.

Electronics pallets are another popular category, often containing gadgets like smartphones, tablets, laptops, and accessories. These pallets can be particularly lucrative due to the high retail value of electronics. However, they also come with a higher risk, as electronic items are more susceptible to damage and obsolescence. Potential buyers need to have a good understanding of electronics to assess the condition and functionality of the items accurately. This knowledge can help in deciding whether to repair, refurbish, or sell the items as parts.

Apparel and footwear pallets cater to the fashion-conscious market, filled with clothing, shoes, and accessories. These pallets can range from high-end designer items to everyday wear. The key to successfully managing apparel pallets lies in understanding fashion trends and seasonal demand. Clothing items often need to be inspected for damage, stains, or signs of wear, which can be time-consuming. However, the potential profits from high-demand brands can make this effort worthwhile.

Home and garden pallets are another intriguing category. They often include a mix of furniture, home decor, gardening tools, and outdoor equipment. These pallets are attractive to those who enjoy home improvement projects or have a knack for interior design. Items in this category can vary significantly in size and weight, posing logistical challenges. However, the demand for home and garden products is consistently strong, making these pallets a steady source of revenue.

Health and beauty pallets contain personal care items, cosmetics, and wellness products. This category is particularly appealing due to the high turnover rate of consumable goods. These pallets can include anything from high-end skincare products to everyday essentials like shampoo and toothpaste. The main challenge with health and beauty pallets is ensuring that the products are within their expiration dates and have not been tampered with. Proper inspection and knowledge of product regulations are essential to sell these items safely and legally.

Lastly, there are specialty pallets that focus on niche markets. These can include anything from pet supplies and baby products to automotive parts and sports equipment. Specialty pallets are ideal for sellers who have a deep understanding of a particular market segment. The focused nature of these pallets means that they can provide a steady stream of products tailored to specific customer needs, thereby allowing sellers to build a loyal customer base.

Each type of return pallet presents its own set of challenges and opportunities, requiring different skills and knowledge to manage effectively. Whether dealing with the broad array of general merchandise or the specific needs of specialty pallets, understanding the nuances of each type can significantly enhance the profitability and efficiency of reselling returned items.

THE RESALE POTENTIAL

The allure of Amazon return pallets lies not just in the thrill of the unknown but also in the tantalizing potential for resale profits. Imagine a treasure chest, each item within a promise of financial gain waiting to be unlocked by the savvy reseller. The landscape of resale potential is vast and varied, a terrain where knowledge, strategy, and a keen eye for value can transform a modest investment into substantial revenue.

When delving into the world of Amazon return pallets, the first step is understanding the assortment of goods these pallets can contain. From high-end electronics and household appliances to clothing, books, and toys, the spectrum is broad. Each category presents unique opportunities and challenges. Electronics, for instance, often fetch higher resale prices but may require more thorough testing and repairs. Clothing and accessories, on the other hand, can be sold quickly and in bulk, though they might not command as high a price per item.

The condition of the items is another critical factor influencing resale potential. Amazon return pallets can include brand-new items, open-box returns, and products with minor defects or damage. Brand-new items are the most straightforward to resell, often fetching prices close to their original retail value. Open-box items, while slightly less valuable, can still command a respectable price, especially if they are popular or high-demand products. Items with minor defects or damage require a more discerning approach; they may need repairs or creative marketing to appeal to budget-conscious buyers.

Market research is a crucial component of maximizing resale potential. Understanding current trends, popular products, and market demand can significantly impact profitability. Utilizing platforms like eBay, Craigslist, or specialized resale apps can provide valuable insights into what products are currently in demand and what price points they are fetching. This research helps in setting competitive prices and ensuring that items move quickly, reducing storage costs and the risk of depreciation.

Effective marketing strategies further enhance resale potential. High-quality photos, detailed descriptions, and transparent communication about the condition of the items build trust with buyers and can justify higher prices. Utilizing social media platforms and online marketplaces to reach a broader audience can also boost sales. Engaging with potential buyers, answering their queries promptly, and providing excellent customer service can lead to positive reviews and repeat business.

Another aspect to consider is the logistics of reselling. Efficient inventory management, safe and cost-effective shipping methods, and a streamlined process for handling returns are essential components of a successful resale operation. Investing in sturdy packaging materials and understanding shipping options can prevent damage during transit and ensure customer satisfaction.

The resale potential of Amazon return pallets also hinges on the reseller's ability to adapt and innovate. Market conditions can change rapidly, and staying ahead of trends is crucial. Developing a niche or specializing in a particular type of product can set a reseller apart from the competition. Building relationships with reliable suppliers and staying informed about upcoming sales and pallet availability can also provide a competitive edge.

In this dynamic and ever-evolving landscape, the resale potential of Amazon return pallets is vast. It requires a blend of strategic planning, market knowledge, and a dash of entrepreneurial spirit. For those willing to invest the time and effort, the rewards can be substantial, turning what was once considered unsellable into a profitable venture.

Chapter 2: Sourcing Return Pallets

FINDING RELIABLE SUPPLIERS

Amazon return pallets requires a keen eye and a discerning approach, particularly when it comes to sourcing from reliable suppliers. The foundation of a successful venture in this domain hinges on the ability to identify and partner with suppliers who are trustworthy, transparent, and consistent in the quality of their offerings.

The first step involves extensive research. This is not just a cursory glance at websites or a few quick phone calls. It demands a deep dive into the supplier's history, reputation, and customer feedback. Online forums, review sites, and industry-specific platforms can be invaluable resources. These platforms often host discussions and reviews from other buyers who have firsthand experience with various suppliers. Pay close attention to recurring themes in these reviews, whether positive or negative, as they can provide critical insights into the supplier's reliability.

Another crucial aspect is the supplier's transparency regarding their sourcing and grading processes. Reliable suppliers should be willing to provide detailed information about where their return pallets come from, how they are graded, and what criteria are used to categorize them. This transparency not only builds trust but also allows you to make informed decisions about the types of pallets you are purchasing. For instance, knowing whether the goods have been customer returns, overstock items, or salvaged merchandise can significantly impact your purchasing strategy and profit margins.

Visiting the supplier's warehouse or facility can be an eye-opening experience. It provides an opportunity to see the operations firsthand, assess the condition of the pallets, and gauge the professionalism of the staff. A well-organized, clean, and efficiently run facility is often a good indicator of a supplier who takes their business seriously and values their reputation. During your visit, don't hesitate to ask questions about their sorting and grading process, as well as their policies on returns and refunds. A supplier who is confident in their product will typically have no issue providing clear and comprehensive answers.

Building a relationship with your supplier is another key component. This goes beyond mere transactions and involves cultivating a partnership where both parties understand and respect each other's business needs and goals. Regular communication, whether through phone calls, emails, or face-to-face meetings, helps establish a rapport and fosters a sense of mutual trust. Over time, this relationship can lead to better deals, early access to high-quality pallets, and a more personalized service.

It's also wise to start with smaller orders when dealing with a new supplier. This approach minimizes risk while allowing you to evaluate the quality and consistency of the pallets before making larger investments. Assess the condition of the products, the accuracy of the descriptions provided, and the overall value for money. If a supplier consistently meets or exceeds your expectations with smaller orders, it's a good sign that they can be trusted with larger, more significant purchases.

Additionally, legal due diligence cannot be overlooked. Ensure that the supplier is compliant with all relevant laws and regulations. Verify their business licenses, check for any past legal issues or disputes, and confirm that they adhere to industry standards and best practices. This step not only protects you legally but also reinforces the supplier's credibility.

In the realm of Amazon return pallets, finding reliable suppliers is a meticulous process that demands attention to detail, patience, and a proactive approach. By investing time and effort into this critical aspect, you lay a solid foundation for a profitable and sustainable business venture.

EVALUATING SUPPLIER REPUTATIONS

Understanding the reputation of suppliers is a critical aspect when delving into the world of Amazon return pallets. The reputation of a supplier can significantly influence the quality of the products you receive, the transparency of transactions, and your overall experience in this resale venture. One must pay close attention to various factors to determine the reliability and trustworthiness of a supplier.

First and foremost, customer reviews and ratings serve as a valuable resource. These reviews, often found on platforms such as Trustpilot, the Better Business Bureau, or even social media, offer firsthand accounts of other buyers' experiences. Positive reviews generally indicate a history of satisfactory transactions, while negative feedback can highlight recurring issues such as poor product quality, delayed shipping, or unresponsive customer service.

Another crucial aspect is the supplier's history and experience in the industry. Suppliers with a long-standing presence are likely to have a more established reputation. They have had ample time to refine their processes, build relationships with customers, and demonstrate reliability. Conversely, newer suppliers might not have the same level of credibility or proven track record, which could pose a higher risk.

The quality of communication from the supplier also plays a significant role. Reliable suppliers typically provide clear, prompt, and professional responses to inquiries. This transparency extends to providing detailed information about the pallets, including the condition of the items, the return reasons, and any potential defects. Suppliers who are evasive or provide vague answers may not be fully trustworthy.

Furthermore, the terms and conditions set forth by the supplier can be telling. Reputable suppliers often have clear, fair policies regarding returns, refunds, and disputes. They are willing to stand behind their products and rectify any issues that arise. On the other hand, suppliers with stringent or unclear policies might be more interested in making a quick sale rather than building a lasting relationship with their buyers.

Investigating the logistics and handling processes of a supplier can also provide insights into their reputation. Proper packaging, timely shipping, and accurate tracking information are indicators of a supplier who values professionalism and customer satisfaction. Suppliers who skimp on these aspects might deliver products in poor condition or fail to meet delivery expectations.

Networking within the reseller community can also be beneficial. Engaging with other resellers through forums, social media groups, or local meetups can provide recommendations and warnings about specific suppliers. These personal connections often lead to more candid and detailed assessments than what might be found in public reviews.

Lastly, it can be useful to request sample pallets before committing to larger purchases. This allows you to directly assess the quality and condition of the items provided by the supplier. It also gives you a better understanding of their grading system and how it aligns with your expectations.

Evaluating supplier reputations requires thorough research and due diligence. By considering customer reviews, the supplier's history, communication quality, terms and conditions, logistics, and feedback from the reseller community, you can make more informed decisions. Ensuring that you partner with reputable suppliers is essential for building a successful and sustainable business in the realm of Amazon return pallets.

UNDERSTANDING COSTS

Amazon return pallets requires a keen understanding of the various costs involved. These costs are not just the initial price of the pallets but encompass a range of expenses that can significantly impact profitability. To truly demystify Amazon return pallets, one must delve into the intricate web of costs associated with this unique business model.

The initial cost of purchasing a return pallet is the most obvious expense. Prices can vary widely depending on the source, the type of products, and the condition of the items. Some pallets may be sold at a fraction of their original retail value, while others might command higher prices due to the inclusion of high-demand or high-value items. It's essential to research and compare different suppliers to ensure you're getting the best deal possible.

However, the purchase price is just the beginning. Shipping costs can add a substantial amount to the overall expense. Depending on the size and weight of the pallet, as well as the distance it needs to travel, shipping fees can vary dramatically. It's crucial to factor in these costs when calculating the potential profitability of a pallet. Some suppliers offer free or discounted shipping, which can be a significant advantage, but it's important to read the fine print and ensure there are no hidden fees.

Once the pallet arrives, there are additional costs to consider. Sorting through the items can be time-consuming and may require additional labor. If you're operating a larger-scale business, you might need to hire employees to help with the sorting process. Labor costs can quickly add up, especially if you're dealing with a high volume of return pallets.

Storage is another critical factor. Depending on the size of your operation, you may need to rent warehouse space to store the pallets and the individual items once they've been sorted. Storage costs can vary based on location, size, and the length of time you need the space. It's essential to have a clear understanding of your storage needs and budget accordingly.

After sorting and storing the items, the next step is often refurbishment or repair. Many items in return pallets are customer returns that may be damaged or defective. Repairing these items can incur additional costs, whether it's for parts, tools, or labor. It's important to assess the condition of the items and determine if the cost of repair is worth the potential resale value.

Marketing and selling the items also come with their own set of expenses. Whether you're selling through online platforms, a brick-and-mortar store, or both, there are costs associated with listing, advertising, and transaction fees. Online marketplaces like eBay or Amazon charge fees for listing items and taking a percentage of the sale price. Effective marketing strategies may also require investment in advertising to attract potential buyers.

Finally, it's essential to account for any unexpected costs. These can include items that are unsellable, additional shipping fees for returns or exchanges, and potential losses from theft or damage. Building a buffer into your budget for these unforeseen expenses can help mitigate financial risks.

Understanding the full scope of costs associated with Amazon return pallets is crucial for making informed decisions and maximizing profitability. By carefully considering each expense, from the initial purchase to the final sale, you can develop a comprehensive strategy that ensures your venture into the world of return pallets is both successful and sustainable.

NAVIGATING ONLINE MARKETPLACES

Online marketplaces stand as vast, bustling bazaars where the digital and tangible worlds converge. These platforms, teeming with a myriad of products and opportunities, are the arteries through which return pallets flow, each carrying the potential for profit or loss. For the uninitiated, navigating these expansive marketplaces can seem daunting, but with a keen eye and a strategic approach, one can uncover hidden gems amid the digital expanse.

E-commerce giants like Amazon, eBay, and Walmart Marketplace serve as the primary arenas where return pallets are traded. Each platform operates with its own set of rules, regulations, and nuances that can either aid or hinder your quest for valuable merchandise. Understanding these intricacies is paramount.

Amazon, the titan of online retail, offers a specialized section for liquidation and return pallets. Here, sellers can find an array of goods returned by customers for various reasons – from minor defects to mere buyer's remorse. The Amazon Warehouse Deals section is a treasure trove for those seeking high-quality items at reduced prices. However, the sheer volume of products requires a discerning eye. Detailed descriptions, customer reviews, and seller ratings are invaluable tools in assessing the potential value of a pallet. Furthermore, Amazon's rigorous return policies and customer service standards ensure a level of trust and reliability that is crucial in this venture.

eBay, known for its auction-style listings, presents a different dynamic. Here, return pallets are often sold by individual sellers, ranging from small business owners to large-scale liquidators. The auction format can be advantageous for those with a keen sense of timing and strategy, allowing buyers to potentially secure pallets at lower prices. However, this also introduces a level of unpredictability. Due diligence is essential – scrutinizing seller feedback, closely monitoring bid history, and setting firm budget limits can mitigate risks. eBay's buyer protection program adds an extra layer of security, but the onus remains on the buyer to navigate the platform wisely.

Walmart Marketplace, though newer to the scene, has rapidly grown into a formidable player. Its structure is somewhat akin to Amazon, with a mix of direct sales and third-party sellers. Walmart's return pallets often include overstock items, seasonal returns, and customer returns. The platform's stringent seller requirements and robust logistics network provide a reassuring backdrop for buyers. Here, the key is to leverage Walmart's extensive product information and customer reviews to make informed decisions. The ability to filter search results based on various criteria can streamline the process, making it easier to identify promising pallets.

Across all these platforms, the importance of research cannot be overstated. Thoroughly investigating the types of products typically found in return pallets, understanding market demand, and staying updated on current trends are all critical components of a successful strategy. Networking with other buyers and participating in online forums can also provide valuable insights and tips.

In essence, navigating online marketplaces requires a blend of analytical skills, strategic planning, and a bit of intuition. The digital landscape is ever-changing, and staying adaptable and informed is key to uncovering the potential that return pallets hold. With patience and perseverance, the bustling virtual marketplaces can transform into fertile grounds for lucrative opportunities.

Chapter 3: Assessing Return Pallet Value

INITIAL INSPECTION

As the warehouse doors creak open, the sheer size of the Amazon return pallets becomes immediately apparent. Mountains of cardboard boxes, each with its own story, stand stacked in neat rows, waiting for their next chapter. The air is thick with the scent of corrugated paper and a hint of plastic, an olfactory testament to the vast variety of items contained within.

The first step is to approach these behemoths with a sense of curiosity and a keen eye for detail. Each pallet is a puzzle, a collection of returned goods that range from the pristine to the peculiar. The outer layers of the pallet often provide the first clues. Boxes in perfect condition might indicate items that were returned simply because of buyer's remorse, while those with dents and tears hint at a history of mishandling or dissatisfaction.

Peeling back the layers of plastic wrap that cocoon the pallet, one begins to uncover the true nature of its contents. The topmost boxes are usually the easiest to access, and they often serve as a preview of what lies beneath. A box might contain a brand-new kitchen appliance, still in its original packaging, or a piece of clothing, hastily shoved back into its bag. Each item is a small revelation, shedding light on the habits and whims of consumers.

The process requires a systematic approach. Each box is carefully lifted and examined. The weight of the box, the condition of the packaging, and any visible markings or labels are all scrutinized. A box that feels heavier than expected might contain multiple items, or perhaps something unexpectedly dense. Conversely, a light box might harbor a delicate item, requiring extra care.

Opening a box is an act of discovery. The flaps are pried open, revealing the contents within. Sometimes, the items are neatly arranged, almost as if they were never touched. Other times, they are a jumble, tossed carelessly back into the box. The state of the items can vary widely – from factory-sealed and untouched to visibly used and even damaged.

Electronic gadgets often come with their own set of challenges. A pristine smartphone box, for instance, might still house a device with a cracked screen. The charger and accessories might be missing, or the device might be locked to a previous user's account. Such discoveries necessitate further inspection and testing to assess their true value and usability.

Clothing items present another layer of complexity. Tags might still be attached, but a careful inspection is required to check for signs of wear, stains, or damage. Apparel, especially, needs to be evaluated on both aesthetic and functional grounds. A designer dress, though seemingly flawless, might have an imperceptible flaw that only a keen eye can catch.

The inspection process is not solely about identifying flaws or issues. It is also about recognizing potential. A seemingly mundane item might have hidden value, be it through rarity, brand prestige, or a unique feature. Recognizing this potential requires knowledge, experience, and a touch of intuition.

Each pallet is a microcosm of the consumer marketplace, reflecting trends, preferences, and the occasional oddity. The initial inspection is a crucial step, setting the stage for what comes next. It is a blend of art and science, requiring both a methodical approach and an open mind. As each box is opened and each item is examined, the pallet gradually reveals its secrets, transforming from a monolithic mass into a collection of individual stories, each waiting to be told.

IDENTIFYING HIGH-VALUE ITEMS

The ability to identify high-value items can turn a modest investment into a profitable venture. The process begins with a keen eye for detail and a solid understanding of market trends, transforming seemingly random assortments into treasure troves of opportunity.

Upon receiving a pallet, the initial inspection phase is crucial. Every box, no matter how unassuming, holds potential. Carefully unbox each item, paying close attention to its condition. Items in pristine or near-pristine condition often hold the highest value, but don't overlook those with minor defects; a simple repair might significantly increase their market worth. Electronics, for instance, are highly sought after, but their value can plummet if they are damaged. Testing each device for functionality ensures that you can accurately market it to potential buyers.

Understanding brand value is another essential aspect. High-end brands in categories like electronics, fashion, and home appliances often retain more value even when returned. Familiarize yourself with these brands and their typical price points. A quick search online can provide a snapshot of an item's current market value, giving you an idea of its resale potential. Recognizing a high-value brand amidst a sea of returns could be the difference between a small profit and a significant one.

Condition grading is an invaluable skill. Items are typically classified into categories such as new, like new, refurbished, used, and for parts or not working. Each category has its own market value, and accurately grading an item helps in setting a competitive yet profitable price. For example, a "like new" item can be sold at a higher price than a "used" one, even if the difference in condition is minimal. This meticulous grading process ensures that you maximize your returns while maintaining customer trust.

Seasonality plays a pivotal role in determining an item's value. Some products are in higher demand during specific times of the year. Holiday decorations, for instance, spike in value as festive seasons approach. Similarly, outdoor furniture and gardening tools see increased demand during spring and summer. Keeping an eye on these trends can help you decide when to list certain items, ensuring you get the best possible price.

Another aspect to consider is the uniqueness of the item. Limited edition products or those that are no longer in production can fetch a higher price due to their rarity. Collectors and enthusiasts are often willing to pay a premium for such items. Researching these niche markets can provide insights into which items are worth holding onto until the right buyer comes along.

Packaging also plays a role in value assessment. Original packaging can significantly increase an item's resale value. It not only adds to the perceived value but also ensures the item is protected during transit to the new buyer. If the original packaging is missing or damaged, consider investing in quality replacement packaging to maintain the item's appeal.

Networking with other resellers and joining online forums can provide invaluable insights. Experienced resellers often share tips on identifying high-value items and market trends. These communities can be a rich source of information and support, helping you refine your skills and make more informed decisions.

Each pallet is a puzzle, with high-value items as the pieces waiting to be discovered. Through careful inspection, market research, and strategic selling, you can unlock the hidden potential within these returns, turning what might seem like a gamble into a calculated and rewarding endeavor.

ESTIMATING RESALE PRICES

Understanding the nuances of estimating resale prices is crucial for anyone diving into the world of Amazon return pallets. The process begins with an assessment of the products' conditions. Items in pristine condition can often be resold at prices close to their original retail value, while those with minor defects or signs of use may fetch lower prices. Thoroughly inspecting each item is imperative to accurately gauge its resale potential.

Research plays a pivotal role in this estimation process. By scrutinizing current market trends and prices for similar items on platforms like eBay, Craigslist, or even Amazon itself, one can gain a clearer picture of what buyers are willing to pay. Tools such as Keepa or CamelCamelCamel can also provide historical data on price fluctuations, offering valuable insights into how prices might change over time.

Another important factor is the brand and model of the items. High-demand brands or models generally command higher prices. Conversely, lesser-known brands may not attract as much interest, potentially lowering their resale value. It's essential to stay informed about popular brands and trending products to make educated pricing decisions.

The seasonality of products can significantly impact resale prices. For instance, electronics and gadgets may see a spike in demand during the holiday season, while outdoor gear might be more lucrative in the spring and summer months. Timing your sales to align with these seasonal trends can maximize profits.

Condition grading is a systematic approach to categorizing items based on their state. Common grades include new, like new, very good, good, and acceptable. Each grade corresponds to a different price range, with new items fetching the highest prices and acceptable items the lowest. Being consistent and transparent with condition grading helps build trust with buyers and can lead to repeat business.

Packaging and presentation also influence resale prices. Items that are well-packaged and presented attract more buyers and can command higher prices. Ensuring that products are clean, free of dust, and presented in their original packaging (if available) enhances their appeal.

Shipping costs and logistics are other considerations that affect pricing. Offering free shipping can make listings more attractive but also cuts into profit margins. Calculating the most cost-effective shipping methods and incorporating these costs into the final price is essential to maintain profitability.

The competitive landscape must not be overlooked. Analyzing competitors' prices for similar items helps in positioning your products competitively. Undercutting prices slightly can attract more buyers, but it's important not to undervalue items to the point where profits are eroded.

Customer feedback and reviews provide another layer of insight. Positive feedback can justify higher prices, while negative feedback might necessitate price adjustments. Engaging with customers and addressing their concerns promptly can enhance your seller rating and, by extension, the prices you can command.

Finally, keeping detailed records of sales and prices helps refine future estimates. By tracking which items sell quickly and at what prices, patterns emerge that inform better pricing strategies over time. This data-driven approach ensures that estimations become increasingly accurate, leading to more successful and profitable sales.

Estimating resale prices is a multifaceted process that requires diligence, research, and strategic thinking. By meticulously assessing product conditions, staying informed about market trends, and leveraging tools and historical data, sellers can navigate the complexities of pricing Amazon return pallets effectively.

CALCULATING POTENTIAL PROFITS

Calculating the potential profits from Amazon return pallets is a crucial step in the reselling business. It involves a meticulous process that requires a blend of research, analysis, and strategic planning. The first step is understanding the nature of the return pallets themselves. These pallets can contain a mix of items, from electronics and household goods to toys and apparel. Each category has its own market dynamics, which must be considered when estimating potential profits.

To begin, one must first assess the initial cost of the pallet. This includes the purchase price, shipping fees, and any additional costs associated with acquiring the pallet. It's essential to keep these expenses as low as possible to maximize the profit margin. Many resellers find success by purchasing pallets during sales or from lesser-known liquidation companies that offer competitive pricing.

Next, the contents of the pallet must be carefully inspected and cataloged. This step involves sorting through the items to determine their condition, functionality, and market value. Items in pristine or lightly used condition will fetch higher prices compared to those that are damaged or heavily worn. It's beneficial to test electronics and appliances to ensure they work correctly, as functional items are more desirable to buyers.

Researching current market prices is another critical aspect. Online marketplaces like eBay, Amazon, and Craigslist are valuable resources for determining how much similar items are selling for. By comparing prices, one can establish a competitive yet profitable pricing strategy. It's important to consider factors such as seasonality, demand, and competition, which can all influence the selling price.

Once the items are priced, the next step is to calculate potential sales revenue. This involves multiplying the estimated selling price of each item by the number of units available. Summing these amounts will give a rough estimate of the total revenue that can be generated from the pallet. However, this figure is only part of the equation.

Operational costs must also be accounted for. These include expenses such as storage fees, listing fees, shipping supplies, and labor costs if additional help is needed. Subtracting these operational costs from the total sales revenue will provide a clearer picture of the net profit.

Another factor to consider is the time investment. Reselling can be time-consuming, especially when dealing with large quantities of items. Time spent sorting, testing, cleaning, photographing, listing, and shipping items should be factored into the overall profit calculation. Efficient time management and streamlined processes can significantly impact profitability.

It's also wise to prepare for potential losses. Not every item will sell immediately, and some may not sell at all. Setting aside a portion of the budget for unexpected expenses or unsold inventory can help mitigate financial risks.

Incorporating these elements into a detailed profit calculation will provide a realistic estimate of potential earnings. This analytical approach not only helps in making informed purchasing decisions but also in planning future investments in return pallets. By consistently evaluating and refining this process, resellers can optimize their operations and achieve sustainable growth in the competitive world of Amazon return pallets.

Chapter 4: Negotiating Deals

BUILDING RELATIONSHIPS WITH SUPPLIERS

Amazon return pallets requires not just a sharp eye for potential treasures but also a solid foundation of reliable supplier relationships. These relationships are the bedrock upon which a successful venture in this niche market is built. The process of developing these connections is akin to cultivating a garden; it demands patience, a keen understanding of the landscape, and a proactive approach.

Firstly, identifying reputable suppliers is pivotal. The marketplace is teeming with vendors, but not all offer the same level of quality or reliability. Research becomes your most valuable tool here. Scouring online forums, industry-specific websites, and social media groups dedicated to Amazon return pallets can unearth recommendations and reviews from seasoned buyers. Trustworthy suppliers often have a trail of positive feedback and a transparent business history. Establishing contact with these suppliers should be your next step, and it is here that the art of communication plays a crucial role.

When reaching out to potential suppliers, clarity and professionalism set the tone for future dealings. Introduce yourself and your business clearly, outlining your interest in their offerings and your specific requirements. Asking pertinent questions about their processes, such as the frequency of pallet availability, the general condition of the goods, and their return policies, can provide insights into their operation's reliability. A supplier who responds promptly and thoroughly is often a good sign of a well-run business.

Building trust is a gradual process. Initial transactions might be smaller, allowing you to gauge the supplier's reliability and the quality of their pallets. Timely payments and clear communication from your end also contribute to a positive relationship. Over time, as trust is established, these initial cautious steps can lead to more significant transactions and even preferential treatment, such as early access to new pallets or customized offers.

Networking within the industry is another valuable strategy. Attending trade shows, industry conferences, and local business meetups can open doors to new supplier relationships. These events provide opportunities to interact face-to-face, which can often lead to more meaningful connections than digital communication alone. Engaging with industry veterans can also offer insights and introductions to trusted suppliers.

Furthermore, consistency in dealings fosters a sense of reliability and mutual respect. Regularly purchasing from the same suppliers, providing feedback, and maintaining open lines of communication can create a partnership rather than a mere transactional relationship. Suppliers are more likely to go the extra mile for clients they trust and value.

Ethical practices also underpin strong supplier relationships. Honesty about your needs and transparent dealings build a foundation of mutual respect. Avoiding the temptation to cut corners or engage in dubious practices ensures long-term success and a good reputation within the industry. Suppliers appreciate clients who are straightforward and fair, and this ethical approach often results in reciprocal behavior.

Lastly, it is essential to remain adaptable and open to new opportunities. The landscape of Amazon return pallets is dynamic, with suppliers coming and going. Keeping an eye out for new, promising suppliers while maintaining existing relationships ensures a steady flow of quality pallets. Building a diverse network of suppliers can also safeguard against market fluctuations and supply chain disruptions.

In essence, the journey of building relationships with suppliers is a nuanced and ongoing process. It requires a blend of research, clear communication, trust-building, networking, consistency, ethical practices, and adaptability. These elements together create a robust framework for sourcing quality Amazon return pallets, ultimately demystifying a complex and potentially lucrative market.

EFFECTIVE COMMUNICATION STRATEGIES

The ability to convey your intentions clearly, negotiate deals, and foster relationships with suppliers and customers can significantly impact your success.

At the core of effective communication lies the principle of clarity. When dealing with suppliers, it is paramount to articulate your needs and expectations unambiguously. This means specifying the types of products you are interested in, the condition you expect them to be in, and any particular requirements you might have regarding packaging or delivery. Clear communication helps avoid misunderstandings that could lead to unsatisfactory transactions or disputes.

Negotiation is another critical component. It's not just about getting the lowest price but finding a mutually beneficial agreement. Approach negotiations with a mindset of collaboration rather than confrontation. Listen to the supplier's perspective, understand their constraints, and express your needs openly. By fostering a respectful dialogue, you can often reach a compromise that satisfies both parties. Remember, building a long-term relationship with suppliers is more valuable than winning a single negotiation.

When it comes to customers, transparency is key. Honesty about the condition of the items you are selling will build trust and encourage repeat business. Detailed product descriptions, clear photographs, and straightforward return policies can help manage customer expectations and reduce the likelihood of disputes. If an issue does arise, prompt and courteous communication can turn a potentially negative experience into a positive one. Address customer concerns with empathy, and offer solutions that demonstrate your commitment to their satisfaction.

Effective communication also extends to marketing your products. Crafting compelling listings involves more than just listing features; it requires telling a story that resonates with potential buyers. Highlight the unique aspects of each item, explain its benefits, and use persuasive language to create a sense of urgency. High-quality images and videos can complement your descriptions, providing a visual assurance of the product's value.

Social media platforms and online marketplaces present additional avenues for communication. Engaging with your audience through posts, comments, and messages can create a community around your business. Share updates, respond to inquiries promptly, and encourage feedback. Building a rapport with your audience can lead to increased loyalty and word-of-mouth referrals.

Internally, communication within your team is equally important. Ensure that everyone involved in the process, from procurement to sales, is on the same page. Regular meetings, clear documentation, and open channels for feedback can help streamline operations and prevent miscommunications.

In the world of Amazon return pallets, where the landscape is ever-changing, adaptability in communication is crucial. Stay informed about industry trends, be open to feedback, and continuously refine your strategies. Effective communication is not a static skill but a dynamic one that evolves with experience and learning.

By mastering the art of clear, honest, and empathetic communication, you can navigate the complexities of Amazon return pallets with greater confidence and success. Whether dealing with suppliers, customers, or team members, the ability to convey your message effectively will be a cornerstone of your business's growth and sustainability.

NEGOTIATION TACTICS

The art of negotiation emerges as a crucial skill, one that can dramatically influence the profitability of your venture. Imagine standing in a bustling warehouse, the air thick with a blend of anticipation and the scent of cardboard and plastic. The pallets, towering enigmas wrapped in opaque film, beckon with the promise of hidden treasures. Yet, without the finesse of effective negotiation, these potential goldmines could just as easily turn into financial sinkholes.

The first step in mastering negotiation is preparation. Knowledge, in this arena, truly is power. Before approaching a seller, it is essential to arm yourself with as much information as possible. This includes understanding the typical contents of return pallets, the average resale value of these items, and the common pitfalls to watch for. Researching the seller's history can also provide valuable insights. Are there consistent complaints about the condition of the goods? Do they have a reputation for transparency and fairness? This background work sets the stage for a more informed and confident negotiation.

As you engage with the seller, the importance of building rapport cannot be overstated. A friendly demeanor, genuine interest in their offerings, and a respectful tone can go a long way in establishing a positive relationship. Sellers are more likely to offer favorable terms to buyers they perceive as trustworthy and pleasant to deal with. This human connection, often overlooked in the transactional nature of business, can be a powerful tool in your negotiation arsenal.

One of the most effective tactics in negotiation is to ask open-ended questions. Instead of focusing solely on the price, inquire about the history of the pallet, the reasons for the returns, and any guarantees the seller might offer. This approach not only provides you with crucial information but also signals to the seller that you are a serious and thoughtful buyer. It shifts the conversation from a mere haggling over numbers to a more nuanced discussion about value and risk.

Flexibility is another key component. While it is important to have a clear idea of your budget and desired price range, being too rigid can be detrimental. Be open to creative solutions, such as volume discounts, payment plans, or bundling multiple pallets for a better overall deal. Demonstrating a willingness to find a mutually beneficial arrangement can often lead to more favorable terms than a hardline stance.

Silence, though seemingly passive, is a powerful tactic in negotiation. After presenting your offer or counteroffer, resist the urge to fill the ensuing silence with justifications or additional points. Allowing the seller to process and respond without pressure can often lead to better outcomes. This strategic pause conveys confidence and patience, qualities that are highly advantageous in negotiation scenarios.

Lastly, always be prepared to walk away. This mindset is not about bluffing but about knowing your limits and being willing to adhere to them. If the terms do not meet your requirements, politely thank the seller for their time and move on. This willingness to walk away can sometimes prompt the seller to reconsider their position and offer more favorable terms.

In the intricate dance of negotiation, each step, gesture, and pause contributes to the final outcome. Mastering these tactics not only enhances your chances of securing profitable deals but also builds a reputation as a savvy and respected player in the world of Amazon return pallets.

SEALING THE DEAL

Negotiating the final purchase of an Amazon return pallet is a delicate dance, one that requires a blend of keen observation, strategic thinking, and a bit of patience. The warehouse, bustling with activity, holds an array of pallets, each a mystery wrapped in layers of cardboard and plastic. The hum of forklifts and chatter of workers provide the soundtrack to this important moment.

Standing before a potential treasure trove, it's essential to scrutinize the pallet with an eagle eye. The condition of the packaging can offer subtle hints about the contents within. Are there tears or signs of rough handling? Such details might indicate the journey the items have taken and their probable condition. A pristine exterior might suggest a higher chance of undamaged goods inside, while a battered one could mean more risks, but also potentially greater rewards for those willing to dive into the unknown.

Engaging with the warehouse staff can be invaluable. These individuals often possess a wealth of knowledge about the pallets, having seen countless ones pass through their hands. A friendly conversation can reveal insights about the origins of the items, the frequency of returns, and even tips on which pallets might be hiding the most valuable merchandise. Building rapport here is not just a courtesy; it's a strategic move.

When it comes time to discuss pricing, having done thorough research beforehand pays dividends. Knowing the market value of the types of items typically found in pallets, as well as the going rates for similar lots, equips you with the knowledge to negotiate effectively. Confidence, backed by data, transforms the bargaining process from a nerve-wracking ordeal into a calculated exchange.

It's also wise to consider the terms of the sale. Some warehouses offer guarantees or return policies, albeit limited, which can provide a safety net for particularly risky purchases. Understanding these terms, and negotiating them when possible, can alleviate some of the inherent risks of buying return pallets. Moreover, if purchasing multiple pallets, seeking a bulk discount can significantly enhance the profitability of the venture.

The moment of exchange, where money changes hands and the pallet becomes yours, is both exhilarating and nerve-wracking. There's an undeniable thrill in not knowing exactly what treasures or challenges lie within. The forklift operator carefully transports the pallet to your vehicle, and as it's loaded, the weight of your decision sinks in.

Driving away from the warehouse, pallet securely in tow, the mind races with possibilities. The road ahead is not just a literal path but a metaphorical one, filled with the potential for both triumphs and setbacks. This is where the real adventure begins—sorting through the pallet, assessing each item's condition, and determining the best course of action for resale or refurbishment.

Each pallet is a unique puzzle, and the satisfaction of piecing it together, item by item, is immense. The process may be laborious and occasionally frustrating, but the rewards, both financial and personal, can be substantial. The key lies in the ability to navigate the complexities of the deal with a blend of caution and optimism, always ready to adapt to whatever surprises the pallet may hold.

Chapter 5: Logistics and Storage

SHIPPING CONSIDERATIONS

Within the vast and intricate world of Amazon return pallets, one of the paramount aspects to consider is the shipping process. This journey begins long before the pallets reach the hands of eager resellers. The labyrinthine logistics behind moving these pallets from Amazon's return centers to their final destination is a process that can often be overlooked, yet it is fundamental to the overall experience and success of engaging in this unique market.

Shipping return pallets involves a complex interplay of various factors including weight, size, destination, and shipping method. Each pallet, a treasure trove of returned goods, is unique in its composition, and this diversity directly impacts how it is shipped. The sheer variety of items within a single pallet – from electronics to clothing to household goods – means that no two shipments are ever quite the same. This variability necessitates a meticulous approach to packing and shipping, ensuring that all items are secured and protected during transit.

The first step in the shipping process is the preparation of the pallet. This involves organizing and packing the returned items in a manner that maximizes space while ensuring the safety of the goods. Careful consideration is given to the weight distribution and the fragility of certain items. Heavy items are placed at the bottom, while lighter, more delicate items are placed on top, cushioned by protective materials. This strategic packing helps to mitigate the risk of damage during the often tumultuous journey from warehouse to reseller.

Once the pallet is prepared, the next decision revolves around the choice of shipping method. Options range from standard ground shipping to expedited air freight, each with its own set of costs and benefits. Ground shipping is generally more economical, making it a popular choice for larger, heavier pallets that are not time-sensitive. However, it also tends to be slower, with transit times varying depending on the distance between the return center and the reseller's location. On the other hand, air freight offers the advantage of speed, ensuring that pallets reach their destination quickly. This method is particularly advantageous for resellers who require a swift turnaround to meet market demands.

The cost of shipping is another critical consideration. The price can vary dramatically based on factors such as the pallet's weight, dimensions, and the chosen shipping method. Additionally, shipping costs can be influenced by the destination, with remote or international locations often incurring higher fees. Resellers must carefully weigh these costs against the potential profit margins of the items within the pallet. In some cases, the shipping cost may be a deciding factor in whether a particular pallet is a viable investment.

Insurance is an often overlooked but essential component of the shipping process. Given the unpredictability of transit, insurance provides a safety net, protecting resellers from potential losses due to damage or loss of goods. Many shipping companies offer insurance options, and while it may add to the overall shipping cost, the peace of mind it provides is invaluable.

The shipping process is a critical phase in the lifecycle of an Amazon return pallet. It requires careful planning, strategic decision-making, and a keen understanding of logistics. For resellers, mastering this aspect is key to ensuring that the treasures within each pallet are delivered safely and efficiently, ready to be transformed into profitable ventures.

WAREHOUSE NEEDS

To effectively manage Amazon return pallets, one must first understand the essential requirements of a warehouse designed for this specific purpose. The heart of this operation lies in a space that can accommodate the sheer volume of returns while maintaining an organized, efficient workflow. The warehouse must be more than just a storage facility; it needs to be a well-oiled machine that streamlines the entire process from receipt to resale or disposal.

Space is the most fundamental element. A warehouse dealing with return pallets must be spacious enough to handle large quantities of goods. High ceilings and wide aisles are crucial, allowing for the vertical stacking of pallets and easy maneuverability of forklifts and pallet jacks. An open layout helps in categorizing items based on their condition, type, and potential resale value. This segregation aids in quick decision-making, whether an item should be refurbished, sold as-is, or discarded.

Beyond space, the warehouse must have a robust inventory management system. This system tracks every item from the moment it arrives until it leaves the facility. Advanced barcode scanning technology and RFID tags ensure that each product is accounted for, reducing the risk of loss or misplacement. Real-time tracking also provides valuable data, helping to identify trends and make informed decisions about future purchases of return pallets.

Lighting and climate control are also vital. Proper lighting ensures that workers can accurately assess the condition of returned items, reducing errors in categorization. Climate control, on the other hand, preserves the integrity of products, especially electronics and perishables. A temperature-controlled environment prevents damage from humidity or extreme temperatures, ensuring that items remain in the best possible condition for resale.

The warehouse must also be equipped with specialized areas for different tasks. Inspection stations are crucial for evaluating the condition of returned items. These stations should be well-lit and equipped with tools like magnifying glasses, testing equipment for electronics, and cleaning supplies. A dedicated refurbishment area is also essential for items that can be repaired or cleaned before being resold. This area should have workbenches, repair tools, and cleaning supplies.

Safety cannot be overlooked. A warehouse dealing with return pallets must adhere to strict safety standards to protect its workers. This includes proper training in handling heavy equipment, clear signage for emergency exits, and regular safety drills. Personal protective equipment (PPE) such as gloves, safety glasses, and steel-toed boots should be mandatory for all employees. Additionally, the warehouse should have fire extinguishers, first-aid kits, and an emergency response plan in place.

Technology plays a significant role in modern warehouses. Automated sorting systems can speed up the process of categorizing and shelving items. Conveyor belts and robotic arms reduce the physical strain on workers and increase efficiency. Software solutions for inventory management, order processing, and data analytics streamline operations and provide valuable insights.

Finally, the human element is indispensable. A well-trained, motivated workforce is the backbone of any successful warehouse operation. Employees should be knowledgeable about the products they handle and trained in the latest warehouse technologies and safety protocols. Regular training sessions and opportunities for professional development can keep the workforce engaged and efficient.

Creating a warehouse that meets these needs requires careful planning and investment, but the benefits are substantial. A well-organized, efficient warehouse can significantly enhance the profitability of dealing with Amazon return pallets, turning what might seem like a chaotic influx of items into a streamlined, profitable operation.

INVENTORY MANAGEMENT

Managing the sheer volume of items within Amazon return pallets demands a meticulous and strategic approach. When dealing with these pallets, the key to maximizing profitability lies in effective inventory management. The process begins with a thorough assessment of the contents, which often includes a wide array of products ranging from electronics to household goods. Each item must be carefully cataloged and evaluated for its condition, potential resale value, and market demand.

The first step is to create a detailed inventory list. This involves unboxing each pallet and documenting every item. Utilizing inventory management software can streamline this process, allowing for more efficient tracking and organization. The software provides a digital record that can be easily updated and referenced, ensuring that no item is overlooked. This digital catalog becomes the backbone of the entire operation, offering insight into stock levels, product categories, and the overall value of the inventory.

Once the items are documented, the next phase involves sorting and categorizing. Products are typically divided into several categories: new, like-new, used, and for parts or repair. This classification is vital for determining the appropriate sales channels for each item. New and like-new items can often be sold through online marketplaces such as Amazon or eBay, while used items might be better suited for platforms like Craigslist or local thrift stores. Items that require repair or are only good for parts can be sold to niche markets or specialized buyers.

A critical aspect of inventory management is understanding the market value of each item. This requires continuous research and monitoring of market trends. Prices can fluctuate based on demand, seasonality, and other factors. Having a dedicated team or individual responsible for market analysis can help in setting competitive prices that maximize profit while ensuring quick turnover. This dynamic pricing strategy ensures that items do not remain in inventory for extended periods, which can tie up capital and reduce overall profitability.

Storage solutions also play a crucial role in managing inventory efficiently. Proper storage not only protects the items from damage but also makes them easily accessible. Shelving units, bins, and labeling systems can significantly improve the organization of the warehouse or storage space. Implementing a first-in, first-out (FIFO) system can help in managing the flow of inventory, ensuring that older items are sold before newer ones. This method reduces the risk of items becoming obsolete or depreciating in value.

Regular audits and inventory checks are essential to maintaining accuracy. These audits help in identifying discrepancies between the physical stock and the digital records, allowing for timely corrections. They also provide an opportunity to reassess the condition of items and make necessary adjustments to their classification or pricing.

Effective inventory management is not just about keeping track of products; it's about optimizing the entire process to ensure that each item reaches its highest potential value. This involves a harmonious blend of technology, market knowledge, and organizational skills. By mastering these elements, one can turn the challenge of managing Amazon return pallets into a profitable and sustainable business venture. Every item, no matter its initial condition, holds the promise of value when managed correctly.

MAINTAINING ORGANIZATION

The sheer volume and variety of items that come in these pallets can quickly turn into chaos without a proper method in place. The key to thriving in this business is establishing and adhering to a robust organizational strategy.

First and foremost, categorization is essential. Upon receiving a new pallet, the initial step should be to sort items based on their categories. This could include electronics, clothing, home goods, and more. Creating distinct sections for each category in your storage area will help streamline the process. This way, when you need to locate or evaluate an item, you won't waste valuable time sifting through unrelated products.

Labeling plays a critical role in maintaining order. Each section, shelf, or bin should have clear and visible labels. This practice extends beyond just broad categories; consider labeling subcategories as well. For instance, within the electronics section, you might have separate areas for smartphones, tablets, and accessories. Detailed labeling ensures that every item has a designated spot, reducing the chances of misplacement.

Inventory management software can be a game-changer in this business. Utilizing such a tool allows you to keep track of every item that enters and exits your inventory. Modern software options often include features like barcode scanning, which can significantly reduce human error. By scanning items in and out, you maintain an accurate and up-to-date record of what you have on hand, which is invaluable for managing stock levels and making informed purchasing decisions.

Photographing items as they are cataloged can also enhance organization. High-quality images provide a visual reference that can be incredibly useful, especially when listing items for sale online. Detailed photos can help in identifying items quickly and accurately, preventing potential confusion down the line. This practice also aids in maintaining transparency with potential buyers, as they can see exactly what they are purchasing.

Regular audits of your inventory are necessary to ensure everything remains in its proper place. Schedule periodic checks to verify that items are correctly categorized and labeled. These audits can also help identify any discrepancies between your physical inventory and what is recorded in your inventory management system. Addressing these issues promptly can prevent larger problems from developing.

Workspace cleanliness cannot be overstated. A clutter-free environment not only improves efficiency but also enhances safety. Clear pathways and well-organized storage areas reduce the risk of accidents and make it easier to move items in and out. Implementing a clean-as-you-go policy helps maintain this standard. Encourage everyone involved in the process to tidy up their workspace after each task, ensuring that the area remains orderly at all times.

Training and communication are vital components of maintaining organization. Ensure that everyone involved in handling the pallets understands the organizational system in place. Regular training sessions can keep everyone up-to-date with any changes or improvements to the system. Open lines of communication allow for feedback and suggestions, which can lead to further refinements in your organizational strategy.

By dedicating time and effort to maintaining an organized system, you lay the groundwork for a successful venture with Amazon return pallets. The benefits of a well-ordered approach are manifold, from increased efficiency and productivity to a more pleasant and safe working environment.

Chapter 6: Preparing Items for Resale

CLEANING AND REPAIRS

The vast world of Amazon return pallets unveils a peculiar blend of mystery and opportunity, especially when one delves into the realm of cleaning and repairs. As each box is opened, a trove of returned items awaits, each with its own story and state of wear. The first step in transforming these items from rejected to ready for resale begins with meticulous cleaning.

In the dim light of a warehouse, the air thick with the scent of cardboard and packing tape, one can almost hear the collective sighs of returned merchandise. Some items bear only minor blemishes, while others require more extensive attention. The key to unlocking their potential lies in the careful application of cleaning techniques tailored to the material and type of each product.

Electronics, for instance, often arrive with smudged screens and dust-laden crevices. A soft microfiber cloth, gently infused with a mixture of isopropyl alcohol and water, works wonders in restoring the gleam to a tablet or smartphone. The delicate process of cleaning these gadgets involves not just wiping away visible grime but ensuring that every port and button is free of debris. Careful handling is paramount, as even a slight mishap can render a device unusable.

Textiles, such as clothing and linens, present another set of challenges. These items often bear the marks of previous use, from makeup stains to the lingering scent of perfume. A thorough inspection under natural light reveals the extent of the cleaning required. Stains are treated with appropriate solutions, from enzyme-based detergents for organic stains to specialized solvents for oil-based marks. Once treated, a gentle cycle in the washing machine, followed by air drying, ensures that the fabric emerges fresh and rejuvenated.

Toys, a common find in return pallets, require a different approach. Plastic and rubber components can be sanitized with a mixture of warm water and mild soap, followed by a rinse with a diluted bleach solution to ensure all germs are eradicated. Plush toys, on the other hand, may need a more delicate touch. Spot cleaning with a fabric-safe cleaner, followed by a thorough drying process, ensures that these cuddly items are both clean and safe for future play.

Repairing damaged items is a craft in itself. Furniture, often returned due to minor defects, can be restored to its former glory with the right tools and materials. A wobbly chair leg might need tightening with a screwdriver, while scratched surfaces can be touched up with wood filler or polish. The satisfaction of seeing a piece of furniture regain its stability and shine is immense, turning what was once considered a discard into a desirable item once more.

In the world of fashion, minor alterations can make a world of difference. A missing button or a loose hem can be easily fixed with a needle and thread, while more complex repairs, such as re-sewing a seam or patching a hole, might require a sewing machine and a skilled hand. Each stitch brings the garment closer to perfection, ready to be worn and appreciated anew.

The realm of cleaning and repairs is an essential aspect of the Amazon return pallets journey. It is through these meticulous efforts that items are transformed, given a second chance to shine and serve. Each cleaned and repaired item represents not just a restored product, but a testament to the value of care and craftsmanship in a world often quick to discard the imperfect.

PACKAGING AND PRESENTATION

The unboxing experience of an Amazon return pallet is akin to peeling back the layers of a mystery, each layer revealing new surprises and hidden treasures. The first layer, the packaging, sets the stage for what lies within. These pallets arrive in various forms, each meticulously wrapped and secured, often with industrial-grade plastic wrap or heavy-duty straps. The outer appearance can be deceiving; a seemingly nondescript pallet might hold high-value items, while an impressive-looking one might be filled with more mundane returns.

Upon closer inspection, the packaging often tells a story of its own. Some pallets are neatly organized, with items carefully placed and cushioned to avoid further damage. Others might appear more chaotic, a jumble of mismatched boxes and items hastily thrown together. This variability is part of the allure, each pallet a unique puzzle waiting to be solved.

The presentation of these pallets can vary widely depending on their source and the type of merchandise they contain. Electronics pallets, for example, might be dominated by a sea of familiar brand logos, their boxes in various states of wear. Clothing and apparel pallets often feature a riot of colors and textures, with garments in every conceivable style and size. The condition of the items can range from pristine, still in their original packaging, to slightly used, with the faintest hints of previous ownership.

Opening these pallets is an exercise in anticipation and discovery. The initial visual and tactile experience can be overwhelming, a sensory overload of sights and textures. Each item pulled from the pallet is a potential gem, its value and condition scrutinized with eager eyes. The thrill of finding a high-ticket item in perfect condition is matched only by the satisfaction of uncovering a hidden gem among the more mundane returns.

The presentation within the pallets also includes the occasional oddity or unexpected item. These surprises add an element of unpredictability, keeping the unboxing experience fresh and exciting. A pallet primarily composed of electronics might yield a random kitchen appliance or a piece of home decor, adding to the eclectic mix.

The process of sorting and categorizing the items from a return pallet is both methodical and exhilarating. Each item is evaluated for its condition and potential resale value. Pristine items are set aside for premium listings, while those with minor defects might be earmarked for discount sales. The damaged or irreparable items are often relegated to the parts or recycling bins, ensuring that nothing goes to waste.

The physical act of unpacking and presenting the items from a return pallet is mirrored by the mental process of envisioning their future. Each item holds the potential for a new life, whether it be through resale, donation, or repurposing. This sense of possibility and renewal is at the heart of the return pallet experience, transforming what was once discarded into something valuable once again.

In essence, the packaging and presentation of Amazon return pallets are integral to their appeal. They represent the first step in a journey of discovery, each pallet a blank canvas filled with potential. The excitement of unboxing, the thrill of the unexpected, and the satisfaction of finding hidden treasures all contribute to the allure of these enigmatic collections. The careful balance of chaos and order within each pallet makes every unboxing experience unique, a testament to the endless possibilities contained within.

CREATING LISTINGS

The world of Amazon return pallets is a treasure trove of opportunities, each box a Pandora's chest waiting to be opened. To transform these hidden gems into a profitable venture, one must master the art of creating compelling listings. This process, though seemingly straightforward, requires a blend of creativity, precision, and strategic thinking.

Every listing begins with a title, the first touchpoint for potential buyers. It must be both captivating and informative, striking a balance between creativity and clarity. Use keywords that resonate with what buyers are searching for, yet ensure the title remains concise and to the point. A title like "Certified Refurbished Apple iPhone 12 Pro Max - 256GB - Space Gray" is more effective than a vague "Smartphone." It tells the buyer exactly what to expect, creating a sense of trust and reliability.

The next crucial element is the product description. This is where the magic happens, where you can truly differentiate your listing from countless others. A well-crafted description should paint a vivid picture in the buyer's mind. Imagine the product in their hands, how it feels, looks, and functions. Highlight key features and benefits, but avoid overloading the text with technical jargon. Instead, focus on how the product can enhance the buyer's life.

For instance, "Experience unparalleled performance with the Apple iPhone 12 Pro Max. Its 256GB storage ensures you never run out of space for your precious memories, while the Space Gray finish adds a touch of elegance to your everyday style."

High-quality images are the visual storytellers of your listing. They should be clear, well-lit, and showcase the product from multiple angles. Include close-ups of any unique features or potential imperfections, building transparency and trust. If possible, use lifestyle images that show the product in use, helping buyers envision it in their own lives. A picture of the iPhone 12 Pro Max on a sleek wooden desk, or being used to capture a stunning sunset, can be more compelling than a simple front-facing shot.

Pricing is another critical factor. Research similar products to determine a competitive yet profitable price point. If the item is refurbished or has minor defects, be transparent about its condition and adjust the price accordingly. Offering a fair return policy can also reassure buyers and increase the likelihood of a sale.

Customer reviews and ratings play an influential role in the decision-making process. Encourage satisfied buyers to leave positive feedback, and respond promptly and professionally to any negative reviews. This demonstrates your commitment to customer satisfaction and can turn a potential deterrent into an opportunity to showcase excellent customer service.

Shipping details and delivery times are often overlooked but are vital components of a successful listing. Clearly state the shipping options, costs, and estimated delivery times. If you offer expedited shipping, make sure to highlight this feature as it can be a deciding factor for many buyers.

Creating a standout listing is both an art and a science. It requires a deep understanding of your product, your market, and your buyers. By paying meticulous attention to each element—from the title and description to images, pricing, and customer service—you can transform your Amazon return pallet treasures into profitable listings that captivate and convert.

PHOTOGRAPHY TIPS

Capturing the essence of Amazon return pallets can be both an art and a science. Whether you are documenting your finds for resale purposes or simply sharing your discoveries with a curious audience, effective photography can make all the difference. The key lies in presenting each item in a way that maximizes its appeal while providing an honest representation.

Begin with the basics: lighting. Natural light is your best friend when photographing items from your Amazon return pallets. Position your items near a large window where daylight can illuminate them evenly. Avoid harsh, direct sunlight as it can create unwanted shadows and highlights. If natural light isn't an option, invest in softbox lighting or LED panel lights to recreate a similar effect. Consistent, even lighting ensures that the true colors and details of the items are visible.

Backgrounds play a crucial role in showcasing your items effectively. A clean, uncluttered background helps to focus attention on the item itself. White or neutral-colored backdrops are often the best choice, as they do not distract from the subject. For smaller items, a lightbox can be a valuable tool, providing both a neutral background and controlled lighting. For larger items, consider using a plain wall or a large sheet of white paper as a backdrop.

Angles and perspectives can dramatically alter the perception of an item. Take multiple shots from different angles to provide a comprehensive view. For instance, a top-down shot might work well for flat items like books or electronics, while a three-quarter angle might be better suited for dimensional objects like shoes or kitchen appliances. Don't hesitate to get close-ups of unique features or any signs of wear and tear. Transparency is key, especially when dealing with return items, as potential buyers appreciate knowing exactly what they are getting.

Staging can elevate the perceived value of an item. Simple props can help convey the utility or aesthetic appeal of a product. A returned coffee maker, for example, might be photographed on a kitchen counter with a few mugs and coffee beans scattered around. Such staging helps potential buyers visualize the item in a real-world setting, making it more relatable and desirable.

Editing should be approached with care. While enhancing brightness and contrast can make your photos more appealing, avoid over-editing, which can distort the true appearance of the items. Basic adjustments can be made using free or inexpensive photo editing software like GIMP or even built-in smartphone apps. The goal is to enhance the image while maintaining an honest representation of the product.

Consistency is another important factor. If you are photographing multiple items, try to maintain a consistent style throughout. This includes using the same lighting setup, background, and similar angles. Consistency not only makes your collection look more professional but also helps in building a recognizable brand if you are reselling items.

Lastly, consider the context in which your photos will be viewed. If you are uploading them to an online marketplace, ensure that the resolution is high enough for clear viewing but not so large that it slows down the loading time. Many platforms have specific guidelines for image dimensions and file sizes, so be sure to adhere to those for optimal results.

Effective photography can significantly enhance the appeal and trustworthiness of items from Amazon return pallets, making them more attractive to potential buyers or followers. With attention to detail and a little creativity, you can transform simple snapshots into compelling visual stories.

Chapter 7: Selling Platforms

ONLINE MARKETPLACES

The digital age has revolutionized the way we shop, bringing an array of products to our fingertips. Among the pioneers of this transformation is Amazon, a behemoth in the world of online marketplaces. The convenience of browsing through millions of items, reading customer reviews, and making purchases with a single click has not only reshaped consumer behavior but also the retail landscape.

Amazon, with its vast and varied inventory, offers everything from electronics to clothing, books to home goods. The platform's sophisticated algorithm tailors recommendations to individual preferences, creating a personalized shopping experience. This immense digital marketplace operates on a level of efficiency and accessibility that traditional brick-and-mortar stores struggle to match. The result is a thriving ecosystem where sellers and buyers from around the globe converge.

The concept of online marketplaces extends beyond just Amazon. Platforms like eBay, Alibaba, and Etsy each cater to different niches and demographics, yet all share the common goal of connecting sellers with buyers in a seamless, user-friendly manner. These platforms offer a stage for small businesses and individual entrepreneurs to reach a global audience, democratizing commerce in unprecedented ways. Sellers can list products with relative ease, leveraging the platform's infrastructure for payment processing, customer service, and even logistics.

Amazon stands out not only for its scale but also for its innovative features. The Prime membership, for instance, offers benefits like free two-day shipping, access to streaming services, and exclusive deals, creating a loyal customer base. The introduction of Fulfillment by Amazon (FBA) has further streamlined the process for sellers. By allowing Amazon to handle storage, packaging, and shipping, sellers can focus on sourcing and marketing their products. This service has been particularly advantageous for small and medium-sized enterprises looking to scale their operations without significant overhead costs.

However, the sheer volume of transactions on these platforms inevitably leads to returns. Whether due to buyer's remorse, damaged items, or simply a change of mind, returns are a significant part of the e-commerce equation. For Amazon, handling these returns efficiently is crucial to maintaining customer satisfaction and operational efficiency. Returned items are inspected, and those deemed resellable are listed again. Others are liquidated through various channels, including Amazon return pallets.

These pallets, often a mix of overstock, customer returns, and occasionally damaged goods, present a unique opportunity for resellers and bargain hunters. Purchasing return pallets can be a gamble, as the exact contents are not always fully disclosed. However, for those willing to take the risk, the potential for profit can be substantial. The items within these pallets can range from high-end electronics to everyday household items, often at a fraction of their retail price.

The secondary market for these return pallets has grown robustly, with dedicated liquidation marketplaces facilitating the exchange. Buyers can bid on pallets, sometimes sight unseen, and either resell the items individually or in smaller lots. This practice not only provides a second life for returned items but also supports a circular economy by reducing waste.

In essence, online marketplaces like Amazon have not only transformed how we shop but have also created new opportunities within the retail ecosystem. The phenomenon of return pallets is just one example of the innovative and dynamic nature of this digital commerce landscape. As technology continues to evolve, so too will the intricacies and opportunities within these vast online marketplaces.

LOCAL MARKETS

Local markets is akin to stepping into a treasure trove of hidden gems. Each stall is a testament to the eclectic mix of items that make up Amazon Return Pallets, radiating a sense of anticipation and discovery. Vendors, with their well-practiced pitches, stand behind tables brimming with an array of goods, from electronics to household items, each piece carrying a story of its own.

The atmosphere is a bustling hive of activity, punctuated by the hum of conversations, the clinking of merchandise being examined, and the occasional exclamation of delight from a customer who has found exactly what they were looking for. These markets are more than just places of commerce; they are vibrant communities where the exchange of goods is intertwined with the exchange of stories and experiences.

Navigating through the market, one can't help but notice the diversity of the items on display. Here, a vendor showcases a collection of slightly used smartphones, their screens lighting up with potential as they are tested by curious buyers. Next to them, a table is laden with kitchen appliances, each one promising to make meal preparation a breeze. The scent of fresh coffee wafts through the air from a nearby stall, adding a comforting aroma to the sensory tapestry of the market.

The sellers themselves are as varied as the items they offer. Some are seasoned veterans of the trade, their stalls meticulously organized and their knowledge of the products encyclopedic. Others are newer to the scene, bringing with them a fresh perspective and a palpable enthusiasm. They engage in animated discussions with potential buyers, sharing insights about the origins of the items and offering suggestions on how they can be used or refurbished.

Customers, too, come from all walks of life. Bargain hunters, tech enthusiasts, and casual browsers all converge in this dynamic marketplace, each driven by the thrill of the hunt. Some are on a mission, moving with purpose from stall to stall, while others meander more leisurely, allowing their curiosity to guide them. The common thread that unites them is the shared excitement of uncovering a great deal or a unique find.

The ebb and flow of the crowd create a rhythmic pulse, a living heartbeat that keeps the market alive. The exchange of currency, the nods of agreement, and the smiles of satisfaction all contribute to the vibrant energy that defines these local markets. Every transaction is a small victory, a testament to the resourcefulness and resilience of both buyers and sellers.

As the day progresses, the market evolves, items finding new homes and new items taking their place. The cycle of discovery and acquisition continues, each market day bringing with it a fresh wave of opportunities. For those who frequent these markets, there is always the promise of something new, something unexpected waiting just around the corner.

In this ever-changing landscape, local markets are a crucial node in the network of Amazon Return Pallets. They serve as a bridge between the world of excess and the world of need, transforming what was once discarded into something valuable and desired. It is here, in the heart of these bustling markets, that the true potential of Amazon Return Pallets is realized, one transaction at a time.

SOCIAL MEDIA CHANNELS

Social media channels have revolutionized the way individuals and businesses interact, share information, and conduct commerce. For those venturing into the world of Amazon return pallets, these platforms offer a treasure trove of resources, insights, and opportunities that can significantly impact their success. The vibrant communities, groups, and forums within social media networks serve as invaluable assets for both novices and seasoned professionals in the pallet liquidation industry.

Facebook, with its vast user base and diverse groups, stands out as a prime platform for those interested in Amazon return pallets. Numerous specialized groups cater to different aspects of the business, from sourcing and buying pallets to strategies for reselling and upcycling. These groups are often filled with experienced members who are willing to share their knowledge, tips, and even cautionary tales. Engaging in these communities allows individuals to stay updated with the latest trends, discover reliable suppliers, and gain insights into the nuances of the market. The marketplace feature on Facebook also provides a localized platform to buy and sell items, making it easier to offload goods sourced from return pallets.

Instagram, known for its visual appeal and broad reach, plays a pivotal role in showcasing the potential of Amazon return pallets. By following influencers and businesses that specialize in pallet liquidation, one can glean innovative ideas for product presentation, marketing strategies, and customer engagement. High-quality images and videos of unboxing return pallets, before-and-after transformations, and creative upcycling projects captivate audiences and inspire others to explore similar ventures. Instagram Stories and Reels, with their ephemeral nature, offer a dynamic way to share real-time updates, promotions, and behind-the-scenes glimpses, fostering a sense of immediacy and authenticity.

YouTube, a powerhouse of video content, is another critical channel for those interested in Amazon return pallets. Detailed tutorials, unboxing videos, product reviews, and business advice are readily accessible, providing a wealth of information to help navigate the complexities of the pallet liquidation business. Channels dedicated to reselling often delve into the specifics of evaluating the contents of return pallets, identifying profitable items, and implementing efficient resale strategies. The visual and auditory elements of YouTube videos make the learning process engaging and comprehensive, allowing viewers to see real-world applications of theoretical knowledge.

Twitter, with its real-time updates and succinct communication style, serves as a rapid information exchange hub. By following industry leaders, liquidation companies, and relevant hashtags, individuals can stay abreast of the latest news, trends, and opportunities in the Amazon return pallet market. Engaging in Twitter chats and discussions can also lead to valuable networking opportunities and collaborations. The platform's immediacy makes it an excellent tool for monitoring market fluctuations and emerging trends, enabling swift and informed decision-making.

LinkedIn, primarily known for professional networking, also offers significant benefits for those involved in Amazon return pallets. Joining relevant groups and following industry experts can provide insights into the business aspects of pallet liquidation, such as supply chain management, logistics, and market analysis. LinkedIn's professional environment encourages meaningful connections and knowledge-sharing, fostering a community of like-minded professionals dedicated to mutual growth and success.

Harnessing the power of these social media channels can dramatically enhance one's understanding and proficiency in the Amazon return pallet business. Each platform offers unique advantages, from community support and visual inspiration to real-time updates and professional networking. Engaging actively and strategically with these channels can unlock new opportunities, streamline operations, and ultimately contribute to a more successful and sustainable business model in the dynamic world of pallet liquidation.

BUILDING YOUR OWN E-COMMERCE SITE

Creating your own e-commerce site is a pivotal step for anyone delving into the world of Amazon return pallets. It serves as the digital storefront where potential customers can peruse your curated selection of items and make purchases with ease. A well-designed e-commerce site not only boosts credibility but also enhances user experience, paving the way for repeat customers and positive reviews.

The foundation of any successful e-commerce site lies in selecting the right platform. There are several user-friendly options available, such as Shopify, WooCommerce, and BigCommerce, each offering unique features tailored to different needs. Shopify, for instance, is renowned for its simplicity and extensive app ecosystem, making it ideal for beginners. WooCommerce, on the other hand, integrates seamlessly with WordPress, providing flexibility and customization for those with some technical know-how.

Once the platform is chosen, the next step involves securing a domain name. This is more than just a web address; it's your brand's identity on the internet. A memorable and relevant domain name can significantly impact your site's visibility and customer recall. After securing your domain, the focus shifts to web hosting. Reliable hosting ensures that your site remains accessible and performs well, even during traffic spikes.

Designing the site is where creativity meets functionality. A clean, intuitive layout with high-quality images and detailed product descriptions can make a significant difference. Navigation should be straightforward, enabling users to find what they're looking for without hassle. Categories and filters can help organize products, making the browsing experience pleasant and efficient. Incorporating customer reviews and ratings can also build trust and provide social proof, encouraging new customers to make purchases.

Payment gateways are another crucial aspect. Offering multiple payment options, such as credit cards, PayPal, and other digital wallets, can cater to a broader audience. Security is paramount; ensuring that your site is PCI compliant and uses SSL certificates can protect customer data and foster trust.

Shipping and logistics are equally important. Transparent shipping policies and multiple delivery options can enhance customer satisfaction. Integrating real-time shipping calculators can provide accurate shipping costs, preventing any unpleasant surprises for customers at checkout. Additionally, a robust inventory management system ensures that you can keep track of stock levels and manage orders efficiently.

SEO (Search Engine Optimization) plays a vital role in driving organic traffic to your site. Utilizing relevant keywords, creating engaging content, and optimizing product pages can improve your site's ranking on search engines. Blogging about industry trends, product usage tips, and other relevant topics can also attract visitors and establish your site as an authority in the niche of Amazon return pallets.

Marketing strategies such as email campaigns, social media marketing, and PPC (Pay-Per-Click) advertising can further enhance visibility and drive traffic. Offering promotions, discounts, and loyalty programs can entice customers and encourage repeat business.

Customer service remains the backbone of a successful e-commerce site. Providing multiple contact options, such as live chat, email, and phone support, ensures that customers can reach out with any queries or concerns. A comprehensive FAQ section and clear return policies can also preemptively address common issues, enhancing the overall customer experience.

Building an e-commerce site demands a blend of strategic planning, creative design, and technical execution. Each element, from the choice of platform to customer service, plays a crucial role in creating a seamless and enjoyable shopping experience. As you navigate through these steps, remember that the goal is to create a site that not only showcases your products but also builds lasting relationships with your customers.

Chapter 8: Marketing Strategies

UNDERSTANDING YOUR TARGET AUDIENCE

To successfully navigate the world of Amazon return pallets, it's essential to first grasp the essence of your target audience. This understanding forms the foundation upon which all other strategies are built. Imagine a bustling marketplace filled with diverse individuals, each with unique needs, preferences, and buying behaviors. This is your audience, and knowing them intimately can spell the difference between success and failure in this venture.

The target audience for Amazon return pallets is diverse, spanning from seasoned resellers to budding entrepreneurs, bargain hunters, and even hobbyists. Each group has distinct motivations and expectations. Seasoned resellers bring a wealth of experience and a keen eye for value. They know how to sift through pallets to find high-demand items, often focusing on specific categories such as electronics, fashion, or home goods. These individuals are looking for opportunities to maximize their return on investment and are adept at navigating the risks associated with buying returned merchandise.

Budding entrepreneurs, on the other hand, are usually new to the game. They approach Amazon return pallets with a mix of excitement and caution. Their primary goal is to establish a foothold in the resale market. They are eager to learn, often seeking guidance and advice from more experienced peers. This group values educational resources and step-by-step instructions that can help them avoid common pitfalls and make informed decisions.

Bargain hunters are perhaps the most diverse group. They are driven by the thrill of finding great deals and the satisfaction of saving money. These individuals often shop for personal use but may also resell items on a smaller scale. They are less concerned with the resale value and more focused on the immediate savings they can achieve. This group is attracted to the idea of getting high-quality items at a fraction of their original cost, making them frequent visitors to liquidation sales and online auction sites.

Hobbyists approach Amazon return pallets with a sense of adventure. They enjoy the process of sorting through items, repairing or refurbishing them, and sometimes even repurposing them for creative projects. These individuals are less driven by profit and more by the joy of discovery and the satisfaction of giving new life to returned products. They often share their experiences and projects on social media platforms, contributing to a community of like-minded enthusiasts.

Understanding these varied motivations is crucial for tailoring your approach to each segment of your audience. For seasoned resellers, offering detailed information on product categories, market trends, and resale strategies can be incredibly valuable. Providing educational content, such as how-to guides and webinars, can help budding entrepreneurs gain confidence and build their businesses. Highlighting the potential savings and showcasing success stories can attract bargain hunters, while engaging content that focuses on creativity and DIY projects can resonate with hobbyists.

In addition to motivations, it's important to consider the preferred communication channels for each audience segment. Seasoned resellers might frequent industry forums and trade shows, while budding entrepreneurs are likely to follow blogs, podcasts, and online courses. Bargain hunters often rely on social media, deal websites, and email newsletters to stay informed about the latest offers. Hobbyists, with their penchant for sharing projects, are active on platforms like Instagram, Pinterest, and YouTube.

By understanding the unique characteristics of your target audience, you can craft a tailored approach that meets their needs and preferences. This deep connection not only enhances customer satisfaction but also fosters loyalty and long-term success in the dynamic world of Amazon return pallets.

EFFECTIVE ADVERTISING

One of the most crucial elements in this venture is mastering the art of effective advertising. It's not merely about making sales; it's about creating a compelling narrative that resonates with potential buyers while building a trustworthy brand.

Imagine a bustling marketplace where sellers vie for attention, each one trying to outshine the other with their wares. In such a competitive environment, standing out becomes imperative. Effective advertising is the beacon that guides customers to your offerings, making them aware of the treasures hidden within your Amazon return pallets.

The first step in crafting an impactful advertisement is understanding your audience. Who are they? What are their interests, needs, and pain points? Delving into these questions helps in tailoring your message to strike a chord with potential buyers. For instance, if your return pallets predominantly feature electronics, highlighting the unique features and benefits of these gadgets can capture the interest of tech enthusiasts. On the other hand, if your pallets contain home decor items, showcasing how these pieces can transform living spaces can appeal to homemakers and interior design aficionados.

Visual appeal plays a pivotal role in effective advertising. High-quality images and videos of the products can significantly enhance their desirability. A well-lit, clear photograph that highlights the product's best features can make a world of difference. Videos that demonstrate the product in use or provide a 360-degree view can further entice potential buyers, giving them a comprehensive understanding of what they are purchasing.

Crafting compelling copy is equally important. The language used in your advertisements should be engaging, informative, and persuasive. It should paint a vivid picture of the product's benefits, creating a sense of urgency and excitement. Phrases like "limited stock," "exclusive offer," or "best deal" can spur customers into action. Additionally, incorporating customer testimonials and reviews can build credibility, as potential buyers often rely on the experiences of others before making a purchase.

Leveraging social media platforms is another effective strategy. Social media channels provide a vast audience base and the tools to target specific demographics. Regular posts, stories, and advertisements on platforms like Facebook, Instagram, and

Twitter can keep your audience engaged and informed about new arrivals and special offers. Collaborating with influencers who resonate with your target audience can also amplify your reach and add an element of trust to your brand.

Search Engine Optimization (SEO) is a critical component of effective advertising. Ensuring that your listings and advertisements are optimized for search engines can increase visibility and drive organic traffic to your store. Using relevant keywords, creating engaging meta descriptions, and maintaining a user-friendly website can enhance your online presence.

Lastly, analyzing and adapting your advertising strategies based on performance metrics is essential. Keeping track of which ads generate the most clicks, conversions, and sales can provide valuable insights into what works and what doesn't. This data-driven approach allows for continuous improvement and refinement of your advertising campaigns.

In the intricate world of Amazon return pallets, effective advertising is the key that unlocks the door to success. By understanding your audience, creating visually appealing and compelling advertisements, leveraging social media, optimizing for search engines, and continuously analyzing performance, you can navigate this complex market with confidence and achieve remarkable results.

UTILIZING SEO

The world of Amazon return pallets is vast and intricate, offering both opportunities and challenges for the savvy entrepreneur. To truly harness the potential of this market, one must not only understand the logistics but also master the art of visibility. In the digital age, this means employing strategic Search Engine Optimization (SEO) techniques to ensure your offerings stand out in the crowded online marketplace.

SEO is the practice of optimizing your online content so that it ranks higher in search engine results, making it more likely that potential customers will find you. For those dealing with Amazon return pallets, this means crafting content that captures the interest of both search engines and human readers. The first step in this process is keyword research. Identifying the terms and phrases that potential buyers are using to search for return pallets or related products is crucial. Tools like Google Keyword Planner or SEMrush can provide insights into popular search terms and their competitiveness. By incorporating these keywords naturally into your website content, product descriptions, and blog posts, you increase the likelihood of appearing in relevant search results.

Next, consider the structure of your website. Search engines favor sites that are well-organized and easy to navigate. Ensure that your site has a clear hierarchy, with categories and subcategories that make sense. For instance, you might have main categories for different types of pallets, such as electronics, clothing, or home goods, with subcategories for specific brands or conditions of goods. This not only helps search engines understand your site but also improves the user experience, making it easier for customers to find what they're looking for.

Content is king in the realm of SEO. Regularly updating your site with high-quality, relevant content can significantly boost your search engine rankings. Consider starting a blog where you share insights about the Amazon return pallets industry, tips for reselling, or success stories from other entrepreneurs. Each post should be optimized with relevant keywords, but avoid keyword stuffing, which can be detrimental. Instead, focus on providing valuable information that answers the questions your potential customers might have.

Backlinks are another critical component of SEO. These are links from other websites to your own, and they signal to search engines that your site is trustworthy and authoritative. Building backlinks can be achieved through various strategies, such as guest posting on related blogs, collaborating with influencers in the reselling community, or getting featured in industry publications. The more high-quality backlinks you have, the better your site will perform in search engine rankings.

Technical SEO is equally important. This involves optimizing the backend of your website to ensure that it runs smoothly and efficiently. Factors such as page load speed, mobile-friendliness, and secure connections (HTTPS) all play a role in how search engines rank your site. Regularly audit your site to identify and fix any technical issues that could hinder your SEO efforts.

Social media can also complement your SEO strategy. While social signals themselves may not directly impact search rankings, a strong social media presence can drive traffic to your site, increase brand awareness, and generate backlinks. Share your content across platforms like Facebook, Instagram, and LinkedIn, and engage with your audience to build a community around your brand.

By leveraging the power of SEO, you can elevate your Amazon return pallets business above the competition. A well-optimized online presence not only attracts more visitors but also builds credibility and trust, ultimately leading to increased sales and long-term success.

LEVERAGING SOCIAL MEDIA

In the bustling digital age, the power of social media cannot be overstated, especially when it comes to unlocking the potential of

Amazon return pallets. These platforms offer a treasure trove of opportunities to connect with like-minded individuals, discover valuable insights, and build a thriving business.

Imagine scrolling through your favorite social media feed and stumbling upon a post from a fellow entrepreneur who has just struck gold with a pallet of returned Amazon items. Their excitement is palpable, their success story inspiring. This is the magic of social media – the ability to share experiences, tips, and strategies in real-time, fostering a sense of community and collective learning.

Platforms like Facebook, Instagram, and Twitter serve as dynamic marketplaces and networking hubs. Facebook groups, for instance, are teeming with enthusiasts and seasoned resellers who discuss everything from sourcing pallets to refurbishing items for resale. These groups are goldmines for learning the ropes and staying updated on industry trends. Engaging in discussions, asking questions, and sharing your own experiences can significantly enhance your knowledge and confidence in navigating the world of Amazon return pallets.

Instagram, with its visually-driven interface, offers a different but equally valuable perspective. Through photos and short videos, resellers showcase their latest finds, creative refurbishing techniques, and even their workspace setups. This visual storytelling not only provides practical insights but also sparks inspiration and innovation. Hashtags like #AmazonReturnPallets and #ResellingCommunity can lead you to a wealth of content and connections that can be instrumental in your reselling journey.

Twitter, known for its brevity and immediacy, is another platform where relevant conversations unfold. Following industry experts, participating in Twitter chats, and keeping an eye on trending topics can keep you in the loop about the latest developments and opportunities in the Amazon return pallet space. The fast-paced nature of Twitter ensures that you receive real-time updates, which can be crucial for staying ahead of the curve.

Beyond these mainstream platforms, niche forums and specialized social networks also play a pivotal role. Websites like Reddit and Quora host communities where in-depth discussions about Amazon return pallets take place. These platforms often allow for more detailed exchanges of information and can be particularly useful for delving into specific challenges or advanced strategies.

Leveraging social media isn't just about passive consumption of information; it's about active participation. Building a personal brand by sharing your own experiences, successes, and even failures can establish you as a credible and relatable figure in the community. This, in turn, can open doors to collaborations, mentorship opportunities, and even exclusive deals on return pallets.

Moreover, social media analytics tools can provide invaluable data on market trends and consumer preferences. By analyzing engagement metrics, you can gain insights into what types of products are in demand, which refurbishing techniques are popular, and how to price your items competitively. This data-driven approach ensures that your strategies are not just based on intuition but are backed by concrete evidence.

In essence, social media is a multifaceted tool that, when leveraged effectively, can transform your approach to Amazon return pallets. It's a gateway to a vibrant community, a source of endless inspiration, and a repository of actionable insights. By immersing yourself in this digital ecosystem, you can navigate the complexities of reselling with greater ease and confidence, turning potential challenges into exciting opportunities.

Chapter 9: Customer Service Excellence

HANDLING INQUIRIES

In the bustling world of e-commerce, where packages crisscross the globe at lightning speed, Amazon return pallets stand as enigmatic treasures waiting to be uncovered. For those daring enough to delve into this realm, the first step often involves handling inquiries with finesse and precision. This subchapter illuminates the crucial art of managing inquiries, ensuring a smooth and rewarding experience for both buyers and sellers.

In the marketplace of return pallets, curiosity is a constant companion. Prospective buyers, intrigued by the potential of hidden gems, often flood sellers with a myriad of questions. Sellers, on the other hand, must be prepared to respond with clarity, transparency, and a touch of savvy. The initial interaction sets the tone for the entire transaction, making it imperative to handle inquiries with the utmost care.

One of the first considerations is the medium through which inquiries are received. Email remains a popular choice, offering a written record of communication that can be referred back to if needed. However, the immediacy of instant messaging platforms or social media channels cannot be overlooked. Each medium has its nuances, and sellers must adeptly navigate these to ensure timely and effective responses.

When crafting responses, clarity is paramount. Buyers often seek specific information about the contents of the pallets, the condition of the items, and any potential risks involved. Sellers should strive to provide detailed, honest answers, avoiding jargon that might confuse or alienate the inquirer. Transparency builds trust, a critical currency in the world of return pallets.

Equally important is the tone of the response. A warm, professional tone can make a significant difference, transforming a simple inquiry into a positive interaction. Sellers should aim to be approachable yet authoritative, demonstrating their expertise while remaining open and friendly. This balance can reassure buyers, encouraging them to proceed with confidence.

Inquiries often go beyond the basic details of the pallets. Savvy buyers may ask about the logistics of shipping, potential additional costs, or the return policy. Sellers should be prepared to address these queries comprehensively. Providing clear information about shipping timelines, costs, and any guarantees can preempt misunderstandings and foster a smoother transaction process.

Moreover, sellers should anticipate common questions and proactively address them in their listings or initial communications. A well-crafted FAQ section can be a valuable tool, offering immediate answers to frequent inquiries and reducing the volume of repetitive questions. This not only saves time but also demonstrates the seller's thoroughness and commitment to customer satisfaction.

Handling inquiries is not merely about responding to questions; it involves active listening and empathy. Sellers should pay close attention to the underlying concerns or hesitations expressed by potential buyers. Addressing these directly can alleviate doubts and build a stronger rapport. Empathy, combined with expertise, can transform a hesitant inquiry into a confident purchase decision.

In the dynamic landscape of Amazon return pallets, the ability to handle inquiries effectively is a cornerstone of success. By mastering this skill, sellers can navigate the complexities of buyer interactions, fostering trust and paving the way for fruitful transactions. The art of managing inquiries, when executed with care and precision, transforms the initial step of the journey into a solid foundation for long-term success.

MANAGING RETURNS

As products make their way back into the supply chain, they pass through a complex process designed to assess their condition and determine their next destination. This stage is crucial for both buyers and sellers, as it dictates the future value and usability of the returned items.

Upon arrival at Amazon's return centers, each item undergoes a meticulous inspection. This step involves a detailed examination to identify any defects, damages, or signs of wear. The goal is to categorize the products accurately, ensuring that each piece is directed to the appropriate channel. Items deemed to be in pristine or near-new condition are often repackaged and resold as open-box or refurbished goods. This practice not only minimizes waste but also provides consumers with access to high-quality products at reduced prices.

However, not all returns are created equal. Some items may exhibit minor flaws, while others might be completely non-functional. For these products, Amazon employs a grading system that ranges from 'like new' to 'used – acceptable.' This classification helps potential buyers understand the condition of the items before purchasing, thus setting realistic expectations and minimizing future returns.

A significant portion of returned items finds their way into liquidation pallets. These pallets are an eclectic mix of products, often sold in bulk to resellers, small businesses, or bargain hunters. The contents of these pallets can vary widely, from electronics and home goods to clothing and toys. Buyers of these pallets often seek to capitalize on the potential for high-value items hidden among the returns, though the unpredictable nature of the contents requires a keen eye for value and a willingness to invest time and effort into sorting and reselling.

To manage returns effectively, Amazon leverages advanced technology and data analytics. Sophisticated algorithms predict return patterns, optimize inventory management, and streamline the process of reintegrating products into the market. This technological backbone ensures that the return process is efficient, reducing the time products spend in limbo and maximizing their resale potential.

Environmental sustainability is another critical consideration in managing returns. Amazon is committed to reducing the environmental impact of returned goods. This includes initiatives to recycle or donate items that cannot be resold, thereby diverting waste from landfills and supporting community organizations. By prioritizing sustainable practices, Amazon not only enhances its corporate responsibility but also appeals to environmentally conscious consumers.

For sellers, understanding the intricacies of Amazon's return management system is essential. By familiarizing themselves with the reasons behind returns and the subsequent handling processes, sellers can make informed decisions about their inventory and customer service strategies. Proactive measures, such as detailed product descriptions, high-quality images, and clear return policies, can significantly reduce the likelihood of returns and enhance customer satisfaction.

In essence, managing returns is a multifaceted operation that balances efficiency, value recovery, and sustainability. It requires a combination of meticulous inspection, strategic categorization, and technological innovation. For those involved in the world of Amazon return pallets, a comprehensive understanding of this process is indispensable. It not only informs better business practices but also unlocks the potential for profitable ventures within the secondary market.

BUILDING CUSTOMER LOYALTY

Amid the bustling world of e-commerce, where countless transactions take place every second, a hidden gem has emerged, offering both seasoned entrepreneurs and curious newcomers an unparalleled opportunity. This treasure trove is Amazon return pallets, a phenomenon that has redefined the landscape of reselling. Nestled within this dynamic ecosystem is the crucial aspect of building customer loyalty, a cornerstone for any successful venture.

The allure of Amazon return pallets lies in their potential to offer a diverse array of products, often at a fraction of their original cost. Yet, beyond the initial excitement of acquiring these pallets, lies the true challenge: converting this opportunity into a sustainable business model. Central to this endeavor is the cultivation of trust and loyalty among customers, transforming first-time buyers into repeat patrons.

Imagine a customer who stumbles upon your online store, drawn by the promise of high-quality goods at unbeatable prices. Their first purchase is a leap of faith, a tentative step into the unknown. The moment they receive their order, the packaging, the condition of the item, and even the small details like a thank-you note, all contribute to their overall experience. This initial interaction is pivotal; it sets the stage for their perception of your brand.

Transparency is a key player in this narrative. Clearly communicating the nature of the products—gently used, returned, or refurbished—builds a foundation of trust. Customers appreciate honesty, and when they know exactly what to expect, their satisfaction levels soar. Detailed product descriptions, high-quality images, and straightforward return policies further cement this trust.

Customer service is another vital piece of the puzzle. Prompt, courteous responses to inquiries and issues can make the difference between a one-time buyer and a lifelong customer. Consider the impact of a thoughtfully crafted email, addressing a customer's concern with empathy and efficiency. This personal touch humanizes the transaction, transforming a faceless e-commerce interaction into a meaningful connection.

Loyalty programs and incentives also play a significant role. Offering discounts on future purchases, exclusive access to new pallets, or even a simple loyalty points system can encourage repeat business. These gestures show appreciation and incentivize customers to return. The excitement of discovering what the next pallet might contain, combined with the perks of being a loyal customer, creates a compelling reason to stay engaged with your store.

Social proof, in the form of reviews and testimonials, can further enhance credibility. Encouraging satisfied customers to share their positive experiences builds a sense of community and trust. New customers are more likely to take the plunge when they see others who have had satisfactory experiences. Showcasing these testimonials prominently on your website can be a powerful tool in building confidence among potential buyers.

Personalization is the cherry on top. Tailoring recommendations based on previous purchases, sending personalized emails, and recognizing significant dates such as birthdays or anniversaries, all contribute to a feeling of being valued. This bespoke approach can transform a transactional relationship into a loyal bond.

Thus, in the realm of Amazon return pallets, where the initial thrill of the hunt is matched by the challenge of building a loyal customer base, attention to detail, transparent communication, exceptional customer service, and personalized touches can weave a tapestry of trust and loyalty. This not only ensures repeat business but also fosters a community of customers who feel connected to your brand, driving long-term success in this unique reselling venture.

REPUTATION MANAGEMENT

Understanding the nuances of reputation management is crucial for anyone venturing into the world of Amazon return pallets. This niche market, filled with opportunities and potential pitfalls, requires a keen awareness of how your business is perceived by customers, suppliers, and competitors alike.

The foundation of reputation management in this context lies in the transparency and integrity of your operations. Customers who purchase items from return pallets are often looking for value but are wary of potential risks. They rely heavily on reviews, ratings, and word-of-mouth recommendations to make informed decisions. Thus, maintaining honesty about the condition of products and the terms of sale is paramount. Misleading descriptions or hiding defects can quickly lead to negative feedback, which can tarnish your reputation and deter future buyers.

Building trust with your customers starts with clear, accurate product listings. Detailed descriptions, high-quality images, and upfront information about any defects or issues help set realistic expectations. Offering a fair and straightforward return policy can also enhance your credibility, showing that you stand behind the products you sell. This level of transparency not only fosters trust but also encourages repeat business and positive reviews.

Customer service plays a pivotal role in reputation management. Prompt, courteous, and effective communication can turn a potentially negative experience into a positive one. Addressing customer concerns and resolving issues swiftly demonstrates a commitment to customer satisfaction. Personalized responses, rather than generic replies, can make customers feel valued and understood. This approach not only mitigates the impact of any negative experiences but also builds a loyal customer base that is more likely to leave favorable reviews and recommend your business to others.

Engaging with your customers beyond the point of sale is another effective strategy. Regular updates, newsletters, or social media interactions keep your business in the minds of your customers. Sharing success stories, customer testimonials, and behind-the-scenes content can humanize your brand and create a sense of community. Encouraging customers to share their own experiences and feedback can provide valuable insights and foster a sense of involvement.

Monitoring your online presence is essential in managing your reputation. Regularly checking review sites, social media platforms, and forums can help you stay aware of what customers are saying about your business. Responding to both positive and negative feedback shows that you are attentive and care about customer opinions. Constructive criticism should be viewed as an opportunity for improvement. By addressing concerns and making necessary adjustments, you not only improve your business practices but also demonstrate a willingness to grow and adapt.

Collaborating with influencers or industry experts can also enhance your reputation. Positive endorsements from respected figures can lend credibility to your business and attract new customers. These collaborations should be approached with authenticity, ensuring that the influencers genuinely believe in your products and services.

Maintaining a good relationship with suppliers is equally important. Reliable suppliers ensure a steady flow of quality products, which in turn helps maintain customer satisfaction. Building strong, transparent relationships with suppliers can lead to better deals and exclusive opportunities, further enhancing your business reputation.

In the competitive market of Amazon return pallets, reputation management is not a one-time effort but an ongoing process. Consistency, transparency, and a customer-centric approach are key to building and maintaining a positive reputation. This not only drives sales but also creates a sustainable business that stands out in a crowded marketplace.

Chapter 10: Legal and Ethical Considerations

UNDERSTANDING REGULATIONS

Anyone venturing into this unique domain must first navigate a complex web of regulations that govern the buying and selling of returned goods. These regulations, though intricate, are designed to ensure a fair and transparent market, safeguarding both buyers and sellers from potential pitfalls.

Understanding the regulations surrounding Amazon return pallets is akin to deciphering a detailed map. The first marker on this map is the Federal Trade Commission (FTC), which oversees consumer protection laws in the United States. The FTC ensures that all sales, including those involving returned goods, are conducted with honesty and integrity. Sellers must accurately describe the condition of the items they are listing, whether they are new, used, or refurbished. Misrepresentation can lead to severe penalties, including hefty fines and legal action.

Another significant player in the regulatory landscape is the Consumer Product Safety Commission (CPSC). This body ensures that all products, especially those that could pose a risk to consumers, meet stringent safety standards. For instance, electrical appliances must comply with specific safety protocols to prevent hazards like fire or electric shock. Sellers dealing with return pallets must be vigilant, ensuring that the items they resell meet these safety requirements. Failure to comply can result in the seizure of goods and other legal consequences.

State regulations also play a crucial role in governing the sale of return pallets. Each state has its own set of rules regarding the resale of goods. Some states require sellers to obtain specific licenses or permits, while others have regulations concerning the labeling and packaging of returned items. Keeping abreast of these state-specific regulations is essential for anyone looking to operate within the return pallet market legally and successfully.

Taxation is another critical aspect that falls under the regulatory umbrella. Both federal and state tax laws apply to the sale of return pallets. Sellers must be diligent in collecting and remitting sales tax, as failure to do so can result in severe penalties. Understanding the nuances of tax regulations, including exemptions and deductions, can save sellers from potential financial pitfalls.

On an international level, regulations become even more complex. Importing and exporting returned goods involves a myriad of customs regulations, tariffs, and trade agreements. Sellers must ensure they comply with international laws to avoid delays, fines, or the confiscation of goods. Familiarity with the Harmonized System (HS) codes, which classify goods for international trade, is essential for smooth transactions across borders.

The rise of e-commerce has also introduced digital regulations into the mix. Data protection laws, such as the General Data Protection Regulation (GDPR) in the European Union, mandate how sellers can collect, store, and use customer data. Compliance with these digital regulations is crucial, as breaches can result in significant fines and damage to a seller's reputation.

Navigating the regulatory landscape of Amazon return pallets requires diligence, research, and a keen understanding of the laws at play. By adhering to these regulations, sellers can ensure they operate within legal boundaries, thereby building a trustworthy and sustainable business. The intricate tapestry of rules and regulations may seem daunting, but they are the foundation upon which a robust and reputable return pallet business is built.

ENSURING PRODUCT SAFETY

When dealing with Amazon return pallets, product safety becomes a paramount concern. The inherent unpredictability of these pallets means that they could contain a wide array of items, each with varying conditions and potential hazards. To ensure that all products meet safety standards before they reach new customers, a meticulous and structured approach is essential.

The first step involves a thorough inspection of each item within the pallet. This process should be systematic, starting with a visual examination to identify any obvious damage or defects. Items should be checked for broken parts, missing pieces, and any signs of wear that could compromise their functionality. Electrical items, in particular, require careful scrutiny; cords and plugs should be inspected for fraying, and any signs of overheating or electrical damage must be taken seriously.

Next, testing the functionality of each item is crucial. For electronics, this means powering them on and ensuring they operate as expected. Household appliances should undergo a series of tests to confirm they work correctly and safely. This step not only helps in identifying faulty products but also builds confidence in the quality of the items being resold.

Sanitization is another critical aspect of ensuring product safety. Items, especially those intended for personal use, such as clothing, bedding, or kitchenware, should be cleaned and disinfected thoroughly. This not only addresses hygiene concerns but also enhances the overall appeal of the product to potential buyers. Using appropriate cleaning agents and methods is essential to avoid damage while ensuring cleanliness.

Labeling and documentation play a significant role in maintaining product safety standards. Each item should be labeled with pertinent information, including its condition, any known defects, and safety instructions if applicable. Keeping detailed records of the inspection and testing processes can serve as a valuable reference if any issues arise post-sale. This documentation also demonstrates a commitment to transparency and customer safety.

For items that do not meet safety standards, there should be a clear process for disposal or recycling. Attempting to sell or repurpose unsafe products can lead to serious legal and ethical repercussions. Establishing partnerships with certified recycling centers or disposal services ensures that unsafe items are handled responsibly.

Understanding and adhering to relevant regulations and standards is also vital. Different types of products may be subject to specific safety regulations, such as those enforced by the Consumer Product Safety Commission (CPSC) in the United States. Staying informed about these regulations helps in ensuring compliance and avoiding potential legal issues.

Training for staff involved in the inspection, testing, and handling of return pallet items is equally important. Providing them with the necessary skills and knowledge ensures that they can correctly identify and address safety concerns. Regular training updates can keep the team informed about new safety standards and best practices.

Through these meticulous processes, not only is product safety ensured, but it also builds trust with customers. Buyers can feel confident that the products they purchase have been thoroughly vetted and are safe for use. This trust is invaluable and can significantly enhance the reputation and success of a business dealing in Amazon return pallets.

ETHICAL SOURCING

Within the bustling ecosystem of Amazon return pallets, the concept of ethical sourcing stands as a beacon of integrity and responsibility. This practice, often overshadowed by the allure of profitability and the thrill of treasure hunting, is a critical aspect that deserves careful consideration. Ethical sourcing refers to the procurement of goods in a manner that respects human rights, environmental sustainability, and fair trade principles. It's about ensuring that every product within a return pallet has a history that aligns with ethical standards.

The journey of a product begins long before it reaches the consumer. From the raw materials harvested, often in far-flung corners of the globe, to the factories where they are assembled, each step in the supply chain holds potential for ethical dilemmas. For instance, electronic gadgets might contain minerals extracted under dubious conditions, or clothing items could be sewn in factories where workers are underpaid and overworked. Ethical sourcing aims to mitigate these issues by promoting transparency and accountability at every stage.

When dealing with Amazon return pallets, the task of ethical sourcing can seem daunting. These pallets are a mixed bag, containing items from various brands and industries, each with its own supply chain complexities. However, there are steps resellers can take to ensure that their practices align with ethical standards. One approach is to research the brands and manufacturers of the items within the pallets. Many companies now provide information about their sourcing practices, and third-party certifications, such as Fair Trade or Rainforest Alliance, can serve as indicators of a commitment to ethical principles.

Moreover, resellers can prioritize transparency in their operations. This involves being open about the origins of the products they sell and any ethical concerns associated with them. By doing so, they not only build trust with their customers but also contribute to a culture of accountability and responsibility within the industry. Educating consumers about the importance of ethical sourcing can also drive demand for ethically sourced products, creating a positive feedback loop that encourages better practices across the board.

Environmental sustainability is another critical component of ethical sourcing. The production and disposal of goods have significant environmental impacts, from carbon emissions to the depletion of natural resources. By focusing on products made with sustainable materials and practices, resellers can reduce their ecological footprint. This might involve favoring items made from recycled or renewable resources, or those produced using energy-efficient methods. Additionally, resellers can advocate for and implement recycling programs, ensuring that products at the end of their life cycle are disposed of responsibly.

The human element in the supply chain cannot be overlooked. Fair wages, safe working conditions, and the prohibition of forced or child labor are fundamental aspects of ethical sourcing. Resellers can support these principles by choosing to work with suppliers and brands that adhere to fair labor practices. This might require a bit more diligence and possibly higher upfront costs, but the long-term benefits, both morally and reputationally, are substantial.

Ethical sourcing within the realm of Amazon return pallets is not without its challenges. However, by adopting a conscientious approach, resellers can play a pivotal role in promoting fairness, sustainability, and transparency. This not only enhances the integrity of their business but also contributes to a broader movement towards a more ethical and sustainable global economy. The ripple effects of such practices extend far beyond individual transactions, fostering a world where commerce is conducted with respect for both people and the planet.

AVOIDING LEGAL PITFALLS

Understanding the legal landscape is crucial to protect your investment and ensure long-term success. This subchapter delves into the essential legal considerations to keep in mind as you venture into the world of return pallets.

One of the primary legal aspects to understand is the nature of the goods you are purchasing. Return pallets often contain a mix of new, used, and defective items. It's essential to carefully read the manifest, if available, to know exactly what you are buying. Misrepresenting the condition of these goods when reselling them can lead to legal issues. For instance, selling a defective electronic item without proper disclosure can result in consumer complaints, returns, or even lawsuits. Transparency is key; always provide accurate descriptions and clearly state the condition of each item.

Another critical factor is intellectual property rights. Many items on Amazon return pallets are branded goods. Reselling these items without proper authorization can lead to intellectual property infringement claims. Brands are protective of their trademarks and patents, and unauthorized resale can result in hefty fines or legal action. To mitigate this risk, consider dealing with unbranded or generic items, or seek permission from the brand owners if you plan to resell branded goods.

Warranty and liability issues also deserve attention. When you resell items, you might inadvertently take on the responsibility for any defects or malfunctions. This is particularly true for electronics, appliances, and other high-value items. Ensure you understand the warranty terms provided by the original manufacturer and communicate these clearly to your buyers.

Offering a limited warranty of your own can also help build trust, but be mindful of the legal obligations this entails.

Tax compliance is another area where many resellers falter. Income from reselling return pallets is taxable, and failure to report it can lead to penalties or audits. Keep meticulous records of all purchases, sales, and expenses. Consult with a tax professional to understand your obligations and ensure you are compliant with state and federal tax laws. Some states also require a resale certificate, which allows you to purchase goods tax-free if you intend to resell them. Make sure you have all necessary documentation in place to avoid complications.

Consumer protection laws are designed to safeguard buyers from unfair practices. These laws vary from state to state but generally require sellers to provide accurate product information and honor return policies. Familiarize yourself with the consumer protection laws in your jurisdiction to avoid potential legal pitfalls. Ignorance of these laws is not a defense and can result in fines or other penalties.

Lastly, consider the legal implications of shipping and logistics. If you are shipping items across state lines or internationally, you must comply with various regulations, including those related to customs, duties, and import/export restrictions. Failure to comply can result in confiscated goods, fines, or other legal issues.

Navigating these legal considerations may seem daunting, but they are essential for running a legitimate and successful business. By understanding the legal landscape and taking proactive steps to comply with all relevant laws, you can avoid common pitfalls and focus on the profitable aspects of reselling Amazon return pallets.

Chapter 11: Scaling Your Business

IDENTIFYING GROWTH OPPORTUNITIES

Within the bustling world of online retail, Amazon return pallets have emerged as an intriguing facet of the e-commerce ecosystem. These pallets, often filled with an eclectic mix of returned items, present a unique opportunity for savvy entrepreneurs. The key to unlocking their potential lies in the astute identification of growth opportunities.

Hidden within the maze of cardboard boxes and packing materials are treasures waiting to be discovered. Each pallet tells its own story, a narrative woven from the choices and preferences of countless consumers. The first step in this exploration is understanding the nature of the returns themselves. Items are returned for a myriad of reasons: dissatisfaction with the product, minor defects, or even simple changes of mind. By scrutinizing these reasons, one can start to discern patterns and trends that hint at broader market dynamics.

Diving deeper, market research becomes a pivotal tool. Analyzing sales data, customer reviews, and product ratings can illuminate which items are likely to be in demand even as returns. Not all returned items are created equal; some retain their value remarkably well, while others might require minor repairs or repackaging. Identifying which categories consistently perform well can guide your purchasing decisions, ensuring that the pallets you acquire have the highest potential for profitable resale.

Understanding seasonal trends is another layer of this intricate puzzle. Consumer behavior is often influenced by the time of year, with certain products enjoying peak popularity during specific seasons. For instance, outdoor equipment might see a surge in returns during the winter months, only to become highly sought after again in the spring. By aligning your acquisitions with these cyclical patterns, you can better position yourself to meet demand when it inevitably rises.

Networking with other players in the industry can also yield invaluable insights. Forums, trade shows, and online communities dedicated to Amazon return pallets are teeming with experienced individuals willing to share their knowledge. Engaging with these communities can uncover tips on sourcing high-quality pallets, effective marketing strategies, and even potential pitfalls to avoid. The collective wisdom of these networks can significantly shorten the learning curve, allowing you to make more informed decisions more quickly.

Technological tools and software solutions further enhance the ability to pinpoint growth opportunities. Inventory management systems, pricing algorithms, and market analysis platforms can provide real-time data and predictive analytics. These technologies enable you to track trends with greater precision, optimize your inventory turnover, and set competitive prices that maximize profitability. Leveraging these tools can transform the process from a game of chance into a calculated business strategy.

Another avenue worth exploring is the refurbishment and repurposing of returned items. Some products might arrive in less-than-perfect condition but can be restored to their original glory with a bit of effort. This not only increases the value of the items but also appeals to eco-conscious consumers who prioritize sustainability. Developing a robust refurbishment process can set you apart from competitors and open up new revenue streams.

In this ever-evolving landscape, adaptability is crucial. The ability to pivot based on new information or changing market conditions can make all the difference. Staying informed about industry trends, consumer preferences, and technological advancements ensures that you remain agile and ready to capitalize on emerging opportunities.

The world of Amazon return pallets is rich with potential, but it requires a keen eye and a strategic approach to truly thrive. By diligently identifying growth opportunities, you can turn what might seem like a chaotic assortment of returns into a lucrative business venture.

EXPANDING YOUR INVENTORY

As you delve deeper into the world of Amazon return pallets, the opportunity to expand your inventory becomes an exciting prospect. Picture yourself exploring a vast warehouse filled with these pallets, each one a treasure chest teeming with potential. The allure lies in the diversity of items you can uncover, ranging from electronics and home goods to fashion and toys. This variety not only broadens your inventory but also attracts a wider array of customers, enhancing your business's appeal.

Imagine the thrill of unwrapping a pallet to find a mix of high-demand products and hidden gems, each contributing to a more robust inventory. The key to successful expansion is strategic selection. Focus on pallets that align with your niche or target market. For instance, if you specialize in electronics, seek out pallets predominantly filled with gadgets and tech accessories. This targeted approach ensures that your inventory remains relevant and appealing to your existing customer base while attracting new buyers.

The condition of items within these pallets can vary, from brand-new to gently used or even refurbished. This variability allows you to offer a range of price points, catering to budget-conscious shoppers as well as those seeking premium products. Consider categorizing your inventory based on condition, clearly labeling items to manage customer expectations and build trust. Offering detailed descriptions and high-quality images can further enhance the shopping experience, making your inventory more enticing.

Exploring different sources for Amazon return pallets can also significantly impact your inventory expansion. Major liquidation companies and online auction sites often have a steady supply of these pallets. Establishing relationships with reliable suppliers ensures a consistent flow of inventory, allowing you to plan and scale your business effectively. Networking with other resellers can provide valuable insights into reputable sources and emerging trends, keeping you ahead of the competition.

Storage and organization play a crucial role in managing an expanded inventory. Efficiently categorizing and storing items can streamline your operations, making it easier to track stock levels and fulfill orders promptly. Utilize shelving units, bins, and labeling systems to maintain order and accessibility. Investing in inventory management software can further enhance efficiency, providing real-time tracking and analytics to inform your purchasing decisions.

Marketing your expanded inventory requires creativity and strategic thinking. Highlighting new arrivals and exclusive deals through social media and email newsletters can generate buzz and drive traffic to your store. Consider hosting flash sales or bundle deals to incentivize purchases and clear out slower-moving stock. Engaging with your customers through surveys and feedback can offer insights into their preferences, allowing you to tailor your inventory to meet their needs.

Diversifying your sales channels is another effective strategy for maximizing the potential of your expanded inventory. In addition to your primary online store, explore selling on multiple platforms such as eBay, Facebook Marketplace, and local classifieds. Each platform has its unique audience, providing additional exposure and sales opportunities. Participating in local markets or pop-up events can also introduce your products to new customers and foster community connections.

Expanding your inventory through Amazon return pallets offers a dynamic and rewarding avenue for growth. By carefully selecting pallets, optimizing storage, and leveraging diverse sales channels, you can build a versatile and attractive inventory that captivates customers and propels your business forward.

STREAMLINING OPERATIONS

Streamlining operations within the realm of Amazon return pallets is akin to untangling a web of intricate processes. The orchestration of these operations demands a meticulous approach to ensure efficiency and profitability. The first step involves developing a keen understanding of the supply chain dynamics specific to returned goods. Unlike standard inventory, returned items present unique challenges, including varying conditions, incomplete packaging, and the need for thorough inspection.

A critical aspect of optimizing operations is the establishment of a dedicated inspection and sorting facility. This space should be equipped with specialized tools and staffed by trained personnel capable of assessing the condition of each returned item. The inspection process must be systematic, with clear guidelines for categorizing items based on their resale potential. Items in pristine condition can be redirected to the primary sales channels, while those requiring minor repairs or refurbishment can be sent to a secondary processing unit.

Efficient sorting is crucial to prevent bottlenecks in the workflow. Implementing a barcode or RFID system can significantly enhance the tracking and sorting process. Each returned item can be tagged with a unique identifier, allowing for real-time updates on its status and location within the facility. This system not only streamlines the internal operations but also provides valuable data for inventory management and forecasting future returns.

The refurbishment process is another critical component. Establishing a well-organized refurbishment line ensures that items needing minor repairs are swiftly processed and made ready for resale. This line should be equipped with essential tools and materials, and staffed by technicians skilled in handling a variety of product types. Clear protocols for each type of repair or refurbishment task can help maintain consistency and quality in the refurbished products.

Effective inventory management is paramount in handling Amazon return pallets. Developing a robust inventory management system can help track the flow of goods, from their arrival at the facility to their final disposition. This system should integrate seamlessly with the inspection, sorting, and refurbishment processes, providing a comprehensive overview of the inventory status at any given time. Automated alerts for low stock levels or excess inventory can help maintain optimal stock levels and prevent overstocking or stockouts.

One cannot overlook the importance of logistics in streamlining operations. Efficient transportation and warehousing solutions are essential for minimizing delays and reducing costs. Partnering with reliable logistics providers and exploring cost-effective warehousing options can significantly enhance the overall efficiency of the operation. Strategic location of warehouses, close to major markets or distribution centers, can further reduce transportation costs and delivery times.

Data analytics plays a pivotal role in refining operations. By analyzing data from various stages of the return process, businesses can identify patterns and trends that inform decision-making. For example, understanding the common reasons for returns can help improve product quality or customer service, thereby reducing the return rate. Additionally, data-driven insights can aid in optimizing the refurbishment process and inventory management, leading to more efficient operations.

Incorporating sustainable practices within the operations can also yield significant benefits. Recycling materials from unsalvageable items and minimizing waste not only contribute to environmental sustainability but can also reduce disposal costs. Partnering with recycling firms or implementing in-house recycling solutions can be valuable steps in this direction.

Each of these elements, when meticulously planned and executed, contributes to a streamlined operation that maximizes the potential of Amazon return pallets. The blend of technology, skilled personnel, and data-driven strategies forms the backbone of an efficient and profitable returns management system.

BUILDING A TEAM

The success of navigating Amazon return pallets hinges significantly on the strength and cohesion of your team. Building a team that can effectively manage the complexities and nuances of this business model requires a blend of diverse skills, dedication, and a shared vision.

At the heart of any successful team is a leader who not only understands the intricacies of Amazon return pallets but also possesses the ability to inspire and guide others. This leader must be adept at making strategic decisions, handling unforeseen challenges, and maintaining morale. They should have a clear understanding of the market, the potential pitfalls, and the strategies that can turn a profit from what others might see as discarded goods.

Equally important is the role of the procurement specialist. This individual must have a keen eye for value, a thorough understanding of market trends, and the ability to negotiate effectively. Their primary responsibility is to source the best pallets, ensuring a balance between cost and potential return. This role requires not just an analytical mind but also a network of contacts within the industry to stay ahead of competitors.

The inventory manager plays a critical role in the team, overseeing the organization, categorization, and storage of returned items. Their efficiency directly impacts the speed at which items can be processed, assessed for resale, and ultimately sold. This individual must be detail-oriented, methodical, and proficient in inventory management software. They ensure that every item is accounted for, properly stored, and easily accessible when needed.

A marketing and sales expert is indispensable in transforming returned items into revenue. This team member should be proficient in digital marketing, e-commerce platforms, and sales strategies. They must understand the target market, create compelling listings, and utilize various channels to reach potential buyers. Their role is to maximize visibility and appeal, turning what might seem like a pile of returns into desirable products.

Customer service is another cornerstone of the team. Handling returns often means dealing with items that have already been through the customer dissatisfaction loop. A dedicated customer service representative ensures that any issues are resolved promptly and professionally, maintaining the reputation of the business. They handle inquiries, process returns, and manage feedback, ensuring that each customer interaction builds trust and loyalty.

Additionally, the team benefits from having a financial analyst who monitors expenses, revenues, and profitability. This individual ensures that the business remains financially viable, providing insights and forecasts that guide decision-making. Their ability to analyze data and predict trends can mean the difference between a profitable venture and a financial misstep.

Lastly, the importance of a logistics coordinator cannot be overstated. This team member ensures that the movement of goods, from pallet acquisition to final delivery, is smooth and efficient. They manage shipping schedules, negotiate rates with carriers, and ensure that the supply chain operates without hiccups.

Each role within the team is integral, and the synergy between these roles determines the overall success. Effective communication, mutual respect, and a shared commitment to the business goals create a cohesive unit capable of navigating the challenges of Amazon return pallets. Building such a team is not merely about filling positions but about finding individuals whose skills complement each other, creating a dynamic and resilient business force.

Chapter 12: Real-Life Success Stories

FROM HOBBY TO FULL-TIME BUSINESS

In a small, cluttered garage, the hum of a computer and the rustling of cardboard boxes created a symphony of possibilities. This was the humble beginning of what would soon transform from a casual pastime into a burgeoning enterprise. The air was thick with the scent of packing tape and freshly printed labels, as the curious world of Amazon return pallets began to unfold.

The initial allure was simple: a hobbyist's thrill of the hunt. Scouring online auctions and warehouse sales, these pallets contained returned items, often a mixed bag of treasures and trinkets. Each box held the promise of discovery, akin to unearthing hidden gems. The thrill was intoxicating. Imagine the excitement of peeling back the layers of bubble wrap to reveal a pristine kitchen appliance, a stack of bestselling novels, or even a high-tech gadget. It was this sense of adventure that captivated many, transforming mundane weekends into treasure hunts.

Yet, as the garage filled with a growing inventory of eclectic finds, a realization dawned. There was potential here, not just for personal amusement, but for profit. The process of sorting, evaluating, and reselling these items began to take on a more structured approach. The hobbyist's eye for value sharpened, identifying which items could fetch a higher price on resale platforms like eBay or Amazon. The spreadsheets grew more detailed, tracking purchases, sales, and profit margins with increasing precision.

The transformation from hobby to business was not instantaneous but rather a gradual shift marked by milestones. The first significant sale, where an item fetched a price far beyond its initial cost, sparked the notion that this could be more than just a pastime. The garage, once a casual workspace, evolved into an organized operation with shelves, bins, and a dedicated shipping station. The hobbyist, now an entrepreneur, invested in tools and resources to streamline the process: a label printer for efficiency, a digital scale for accuracy, and software to manage inventory.

Networking played a crucial role in this transition. Connecting with other enthusiasts and business owners provided invaluable insights and strategies. Online forums and social media groups became virtual meeting places where tips were exchanged, and success stories shared. These interactions fostered a sense of community and offered practical advice on navigating the complexities of sourcing, pricing, and customer service.

The learning curve was steep but rewarding. Understanding market trends, mastering the art of negotiation, and honing skills in customer relations were all part of the journey. Mistakes were made, lessons were learned, and the business acumen grew stronger with each challenge faced. The initial trepidation gave way to confidence as the operation expanded. What started as a side hustle began to demand more time and attention, eventually leading to the decision to take it full-time.

The garage, once a symbol of a hobbyist's playground, now stood as the headquarters of a thriving business. The transformation was complete, marked by a blend of passion, perseverance, and a keen eye for opportunity. The venture into Amazon return pallets had demystified itself, revealing not just a lucrative business model but a fulfilling career path that turned curiosity into commerce. The journey from hobby to full-time business was a testament to the possibilities that lie hidden in the most unexpected places, waiting to be discovered and nurtured into success.

OVERCOMING CHALLENGES

One of the primary hurdles faced by newcomers is understanding the sheer volume and variety of items that can be found in these pallets. Each pallet is a mixed bag of surprises, ranging from electronics to household goods, all in varying conditions. This unpredictability can be overwhelming, especially for those who are just starting out. However, with careful planning and a keen eye for detail, one can turn this challenge into an opportunity.

Thorough inspection is crucial. Before committing to a purchase, it's essential to scrutinize the manifest, if available, which lists the items included in the pallet. Not all pallets come with manifests, and this adds an element of risk. In such cases, it's wise to start with smaller, less expensive pallets to get a feel for the process. Building a relationship with reputable suppliers can also provide some assurance regarding the quality and content of the pallets.

Another significant challenge is the condition of the items. Return pallets often contain products that range from brand new to slightly used, or even damaged. Developing a systematic approach to sorting and testing these items is key. Setting up a dedicated space for inspection and repair can streamline this process. Investing in basic repair tools and learning some DIY repair skills can also be beneficial. For items that are beyond repair, considering recycling or selling parts can help recoup some of the costs.

Storage and organization pose another set of challenges. As the number of pallets purchased increases, so does the need for adequate storage space. A clutter-free, organized workspace not only makes the sorting process more efficient but also helps in keeping track of inventory. Utilizing shelving units, clear bins, and labeling systems can greatly enhance organization. Additionally, implementing an inventory management system, whether it's a simple spreadsheet or a more sophisticated software, can help keep track of stock levels and sales.

Market research is indispensable. Understanding the demand for different types of products can guide purchasing decisions. Platforms like eBay, Amazon, and local marketplaces can provide insights into what items are currently in demand and their average selling prices. This knowledge can help in making informed decisions about which pallets to buy and how to price the items for resale.

Shipping and logistics are other areas where challenges can arise. The cost and method of shipping can significantly impact profitability. Negotiating rates with shipping carriers or using bulk shipping options can reduce costs. Offering local pickup or delivery can also be a viable option to save on shipping fees and attract local customers.

Customer service is paramount. Dealing with returns, refunds, and inquiries efficiently can build a positive reputation and encourage repeat business. Clear communication, prompt responses, and a fair return policy can enhance customer satisfaction.

In essence, while the world of Amazon return pallets presents several challenges, these can be navigated with strategic planning and a proactive approach. By focusing on thorough inspection, efficient organization, market research, cost-effective shipping, and excellent customer service, one can turn these challenges into stepping stones for success.

INNOVATIVE STRATEGIES

Amazon return pallets have long been a topic of intrigue for many entrepreneurs and resellers. The allure of uncovering valuable items within these mixed lots of returned merchandise drives innovative strategies that can turn potential risks into profitable ventures. To navigate this landscape successfully, one must employ a blend of creativity, analytical thinking, and keen market awareness.

A crucial strategy involves meticulous research before purchasing a pallet. Understanding market trends and consumer demand is paramount. Tools such as Google Trends, eBay's completed listings, and Amazon's Best Sellers lists provide valuable insights into which products are currently in high demand. This data allows buyers to make informed decisions about which pallets are likely to yield the most profitable items. Additionally, joining online forums and social media groups dedicated to reselling can offer firsthand accounts and tips from experienced individuals in the field.

Another innovative approach is the categorization and segmentation of items within a pallet. Once a pallet is acquired, sorting the items into categories based on their condition, brand, and type can streamline the resale process. High-ticket items in excellent condition can be sold individually on platforms like eBay or Amazon, maximizing profit margins. On the other hand, items with minor defects or those that belong to less popular categories can be bundled together and sold as a lot, appealing to bargain hunters and other resellers looking for inventory.

Leveraging multiple sales channels is also a strategic move. While online marketplaces like eBay and Amazon are popular choices, diversifying where items are sold can mitigate risks and expand reach. Local selling platforms such as Facebook Marketplace,

Craigslist, and local flea markets can attract buyers who prefer to see items in person before purchasing. Moreover, these avenues often have lower fees compared to major online marketplaces, potentially increasing overall profitability.

Investing in repair and refurbishment is another tactic that can significantly enhance the value of return pallet items. Simple fixes, such as cleaning, replacing missing parts, or minor repairs, can transform an otherwise unsellable item into a desirable product. For those willing to learn, acquiring basic repair skills can be a game-changer. Online tutorials and courses can provide the necessary knowledge to refurbish electronics, furniture, or other high-value items, thus increasing their resale value.

Building a brand around selling return pallet items can also be an effective strategy. Establishing a reputation for providing quality products and excellent customer service can lead to repeat customers and word-of-mouth referrals. Creating a professional online presence through a dedicated website or social media accounts can enhance credibility and attract a loyal customer base. Engaging content, such as unboxing videos, refurbishment tutorials, and behind-the-scenes looks at the reselling process, can also drive traffic and interest to the brand.

Lastly, maintaining an organized and efficient workflow is essential. Implementing inventory management systems, whether through software or manual methods, helps keep track of stock, sales, and profits. Time management tools can assist in balancing the various aspects of the business, from sourcing pallets and refurbishing items to listing products and handling customer inquiries.

The world of Amazon return pallets is rife with opportunities for those willing to think outside the box and adopt innovative strategies. By conducting thorough research, diversifying sales channels, investing in refurbishment, building a brand, and maintaining organization, resellers can turn the uncertainty of return pallets into a lucrative business venture.

LESSONS LEARNED

Each pallet, a microcosm of the broader world of e-commerce, holds lessons that can reshape how we perceive value, risk, and opportunity.

The first and perhaps most striking realization is the unpredictability inherent in these pallets. Every box is a Pandora's Box, where anticipation meets reality in the most unexpected ways. The sheer variety of items, ranging from the mundane to the extraordinary, teaches a profound lesson in adaptability. One must be prepared to pivot quickly, making swift decisions on whether an item is worth salvaging, repairing, or discarding. This constant exercise in decision-making builds a unique resilience, fostering a mindset that is both pragmatic and opportunistic.

Quality assessment becomes an art form in this arena. The ability to discern the diamond in the rough is not merely a skill but a necessity. This requires a keen eye and a methodical approach to inspecting each item. Learning to gauge the condition, potential resale value, and the effort required for refurbishment is an ongoing process. Over time, this hones one's analytical abilities, transforming uncertainty into calculated risk.

Financial acumen is another critical takeaway. Managing the economics of return pallets demands a fine balance between cost and potential profit. Each pallet represents an investment, and the returns can be as volatile as the stock market. Budgeting, forecasting, and maintaining a healthy cash flow are imperative. The experience teaches one to be frugal yet bold, understanding that every expenditure must be weighed against potential gains. This financial discipline is invaluable, extending its benefits to other areas of business and personal finance.

There is also a lesson in sustainability. Many of the items found in return pallets can be refurbished, repurposed, or recycled, reducing waste and promoting a circular economy. This aspect of the process fosters a deeper appreciation for the value of goods, encouraging a more conscientious approach to consumption and disposal. By breathing new life into returned items, one contributes to a more sustainable model of commerce.

Networking emerges as another essential element. Engaging with a community of like-minded individuals—whether through online forums, local meetups, or industry events—provides a wealth of shared knowledge and experience. These interactions offer practical tips, support, and sometimes collaboration opportunities. The collective wisdom of the community can be a guiding light, helping to navigate the complexities and nuances of the trade.

Patience and perseverance are virtues that are continually tested and strengthened. The process is seldom smooth; it is riddled with challenges, from logistical hiccups to unexpected losses. Each obstacle encountered and overcome adds a layer of fortitude. This journey is a testament to the power of persistence, underscoring the importance of staying the course even when immediate results are not forthcoming.

Ultimately, dealing with Amazon return pallets is a multifaceted endeavor that extends beyond commerce. It is a holistic experience that cultivates a diverse skill set, from critical thinking and financial management to sustainability and community building. These lessons, learned through hands-on experience and continuous adaptation, provide a robust foundation for anyone looking to delve into the world of liquidation and beyond.

Chapter 13: Future Trends in Return Pallets

EMERGING MARKETPLACES

In the global commerce, where countless transactions weave the fabric of our daily lives, a new phenomenon has emerged with the potential to reshape the retail landscape: Amazon return pallets. These are the byproducts of the modern consumer's penchant for online shopping, where items are purchased, tried, and often sent back for myriad reasons. These returned items, grouped into pallets, represent a treasure trove of opportunity for savvy entrepreneurs and curious buyers alike.

Imagine a bustling marketplace, not unlike the ancient bazaars of old, but entirely virtual. Here, the goods on offer are as diverse as the shoppers themselves—electronics, clothing, household items, and more. Each return pallet is a microcosm of this marketplace, a snapshot of consumer preferences and behaviors. The contents are unpredictable, a mix of the new, the gently used, and occasionally, the damaged. This unpredictability is part of the allure, a gamble that can yield incredible rewards or, sometimes, disappointing surprises.

The rise of these return pallets can be traced back to the exponential growth of e-commerce, particularly platforms like Amazon, which dominate the online shopping world. With millions of products sold daily, the volume of returns is staggering. In many cases, it is more cost-effective for retailers to liquidate these returns in bulk rather than reintegrate them into their inventory. This creates a unique secondary market, where return pallets are sold at a fraction of their original value.

This burgeoning market has attracted a diverse array of participants. Entrepreneurs see an opportunity to acquire inventory at low cost, resell individual items, and potentially realize significant profits. Hobbyists and bargain hunters are drawn by the thrill of discovery, the possibility of uncovering hidden gems among the returned goods. For some, it becomes a side hustle, a way to supplement their income while indulging in the excitement of the hunt.

Navigating this market, however, requires a keen eye and a strategic approach. Not all pallets are created equal, and the contents can vary widely in quality and value. Successful buyers often develop relationships with reputable liquidators, gaining insights into which pallets are likely to offer the best returns. They learn to read between the lines of pallet descriptions, to spot the telltale signs of high-value items or, conversely, red flags that suggest a pallet might be more trouble than it's worth.

The logistics of acquiring and reselling these items also present challenges. Buyers must consider storage space, shipping costs, and the time investment required to sort, test, and list items for resale. For those who master these logistical hurdles, the payoff can be substantial. The secondary market for returned goods is robust, with platforms like eBay, Craigslist, and Facebook Marketplace providing avenues to reach eager buyers.

In this dynamic environment, the concept of value takes on new dimensions. An item that was once deemed undesirable by its original owner can find new life with someone else, creating a cycle of reuse and sustainability. This aspect of the return pallet market resonates with contemporary values of resourcefulness and environmental consciousness.

As the market for Amazon return pallets continues to evolve, it reflects broader trends in consumer behavior and retail. It embodies the intersection of technology, commerce, and human ingenuity, offering a glimpse into the future of shopping and the endless possibilities that lie within returned goods.

TECHNOLOGICAL ADVANCES

The landscape of Amazon return pallets has been significantly transformed by the rapid pace of technological advances. These innovations have not only streamlined the process of managing returned goods but also opened new avenues for businesses and individual resellers to maximize their profits. At the heart of this revolution are sophisticated software systems that can analyze and categorize returned items with remarkable accuracy. These systems employ advanced algorithms and machine learning techniques to assess the condition of each product, label it accordingly, and determine the best course of action—whether it be restocking, refurbishing, or recycling.

One of the most striking advancements is the integration of Artificial Intelligence (AI) into the return process. AI-powered tools can predict the likelihood of a product being returned based on previous customer behavior, product reviews, and other data points. This predictive capability allows sellers to anticipate returns and manage their inventory more efficiently. Additionally, AI can assist in the refurbishment process by identifying common issues with returned products and suggesting the most effective repairs. This ensures that refurbished items meet quality standards and can be resold at a competitive price.

Automation has also played a crucial role in revolutionizing the handling of Amazon return pallets. Automated sorting systems equipped with conveyor belts, scanners, and robotic arms can process returns at a speed and accuracy that manual labor cannot match. These systems can sort items based on size, weight, and condition, significantly reducing the time and effort required to manage large volumes of returned products. This increased efficiency not only benefits the sellers but also enhances the overall customer experience by ensuring quicker refunds and exchanges.

The advent of blockchain technology has introduced a new level of transparency and security in the management of return pallets. Blockchain provides an immutable ledger that records every transaction and movement of a product from the moment it is returned to its eventual resale or disposal. This transparency helps to build trust between sellers and buyers, as it ensures that the history of each item is verifiable and tamper-proof. Furthermore, blockchain can streamline the process of issuing refunds and managing disputes, as all relevant information is readily accessible and transparent.

Mobile technology has also made significant contributions to the efficiency of handling Amazon return pallets. Mobile apps equipped with barcode scanners and inventory management features allow sellers to quickly log returned items and update their status in real-time. These apps can also provide valuable insights into return trends, helping sellers to make informed decisions about their inventory and pricing strategies. The convenience of mobile technology ensures that sellers can manage returns from anywhere, at any time, further enhancing their operational flexibility.

E-commerce platforms specifically designed for the resale of returned goods have emerged as a direct result of these technological advances. These platforms provide a marketplace where sellers can list their returned items, often with detailed descriptions and condition reports generated by AI and automation tools. Buyers, in turn, can browse these listings with confidence, knowing that the items have been accurately assessed and categorized. This has created a thriving secondary market for returned goods, where both sellers and buyers can benefit from reduced prices and increased availability.

In essence, technological advances have demystified the complexities of Amazon return pallets, transforming what was once a cumbersome process into a streamlined and profitable endeavor. Through AI, automation, blockchain, and mobile technology, the management of returned goods has reached new heights of efficiency and transparency. These innovations continue to evolve, promising even greater improvements in the future and solidifying the role of technology as a pivotal force in the world of e-commerce returns.

CHANGING CONSUMER BEHAVIOR

The landscape of consumer behavior has undergone a remarkable transformation in recent years, driven by the rise of e-commerce and the ever-evolving digital marketplace. The convenience of online shopping has redefined how consumers interact with products, shifting away from traditional brick-and-mortar stores to the virtual aisles of the internet. This shift has had profound implications for the dynamics of the retail industry, particularly in the realm of Amazon return pallets.

Consumers today are more empowered than ever before. The digital age has brought with it a wealth of information at their fingertips, allowing them to make more informed decisions. Reviews, ratings, and detailed product descriptions provide a comprehensive understanding of what to expect, reducing the uncertainty that once plagued online shopping. This newfound confidence has led to an uptick in online purchases, but it has also contributed to an increase in returns. The ease of returning items has become a critical factor in purchasing decisions, with many consumers viewing it as a safety net that allows them to shop without fear of making a wrong choice.

The psychology behind returns is multi-faceted. On one hand, the tactile experience of shopping is lost in the digital realm. Consumers can no longer feel the fabric of a dress, test the weight of a gadget, or gauge the true color of an accessory through a screen. This sensory deprivation leads to a higher likelihood of dissatisfaction upon receiving the product, prompting returns. On the other hand, the trend of "bracketing" has emerged, where consumers purchase multiple variations of an item with the intention of keeping one and returning the rest. This behavior, while convenient for the consumer, creates a significant challenge for retailers and contributes to the growing volume of return pallets.

Retailers have responded to these changes with varying strategies. Some have implemented more lenient return policies, recognizing that a hassle-free return process can enhance customer loyalty and encourage repeat business. Others have invested in technology to bridge the sensory gap, utilizing augmented reality and virtual try-ons to provide a more immersive shopping experience. Despite these efforts, the reality remains that a substantial portion of online purchases will inevitably be returned.

The implications of changing consumer behavior extend beyond the immediate impact of returns. The secondary market for returned goods, particularly Amazon return pallets, has seen substantial growth. Entrepreneurs and small business owners have capitalized on this trend, purchasing return pallets at a fraction of the original retail price and reselling the items through various channels. This practice not only provides an opportunity for profit but also contributes to the circular economy by giving returned products a second life.

The environmental aspect of returns cannot be overlooked. The increase in online shopping and subsequent returns has led to a rise in packaging waste and carbon emissions from transportation. Retailers are becoming more aware of their environmental footprint and are exploring sustainable practices to mitigate these effects. From eco-friendly packaging to more efficient logistics, the industry is gradually shifting towards a more sustainable model.

Consumer behavior is a dynamic and ever-changing force that continues to shape the retail landscape. As technology advances and consumer expectations evolve, the industry must adapt to meet these new demands. The phenomenon of Amazon return pallets is a testament to the complexities and opportunities that arise from this ongoing transformation. Understanding these behavioral shifts is crucial for anyone looking to navigate the world of return pallets and capitalize on the potential they hold.

SUSTAINABLE PRACTICES

Amidst the bustling world of Amazon return pallets, a movement towards sustainable practices is quietly gaining momentum. These pallets, once seen as mere collections of discarded items, are now being reimagined through a lens of environmental stewardship. The lifecycle of each product, from its initial manufacturing to its eventual return, is scrutinized for opportunities to minimize waste and maximize reuse.

The first step in this sustainable approach involves the careful sorting and evaluation of returned items. Instead of discarding products that are deemed unsellable, companies are increasingly investing in refurbishment processes. Skilled technicians repair and restore these products to a like-new condition, extending their lifecycle and reducing the need for new resources. This practice not only diverts waste from landfills but also offers consumers high-quality goods at a fraction of the cost.

Recycling plays a pivotal role in the sustainable management of return pallets. Materials such as plastics, metals, and electronics are meticulously separated and sent to specialized recycling facilities. Here, they are transformed into raw materials that can be used to manufacture new products. This closed-loop system significantly reduces the environmental footprint of each item, conserving natural resources and decreasing greenhouse gas emissions.

Another innovative approach is the upcycling of returned products. Creative entrepreneurs and small businesses see potential in items that might otherwise be discarded. Furniture, clothing, and even electronics are given new life through imaginative redesigns and repurposing. This not only keeps them out of the waste stream but also creates unique, one-of-a-kind products that appeal to eco-conscious consumers.

Packaging, often overlooked in discussions of sustainability, is also receiving attention. Companies are exploring ways to reduce packaging waste associated with return pallets. This includes using recyclable or biodegradable materials, designing packaging that can be easily reused, and minimizing excess packaging. By addressing the packaging issue, businesses can significantly reduce the overall environmental impact of their operations.

Consumer education is another critical component of sustainable practices in the realm of Amazon return pallets. By raising awareness about the benefits of refurbished and upcycled products, companies can shift consumer perceptions and drive demand for these eco-friendly alternatives. Informative labeling, marketing campaigns, and transparent communication about the environmental benefits of these practices can empower consumers to make more sustainable choices.

Partnerships and collaborations are also essential in fostering sustainable practices. Retailers, manufacturers, and recycling facilities are working together to create more efficient and environmentally friendly processes. These collaborations facilitate the sharing of best practices, technological advancements, and innovative solutions that can be scaled across the industry.

The economic benefits of sustainable practices should not be underestimated. By reducing waste and optimizing resource use, companies can achieve significant cost savings. These savings can then be reinvested in further sustainability initiatives, creating a positive feedback loop that benefits both the environment and the bottom line.

In this evolving landscape, the importance of continuous improvement cannot be overstated. Sustainable practices are not static; they require ongoing assessment and adaptation. By staying informed about the latest developments in sustainability and being willing to innovate, businesses can ensure that their approach to Amazon return pallets remains both effective and responsible.

The shift towards sustainable practices in the management of Amazon return pallets represents a profound change in how we view and interact with consumer goods. It is a testament to the power of innovation and collaboration in addressing one of the most pressing challenges of our time: creating a more sustainable future for all.

Manufactured by Amazon.ca
Bolton, ON